SHOOTING

This book has been written by experts with the express purpose of serving as an introduction to shooting with rifles, pistols and shotguns. It contains a wealth of basic information and guidance, and is liberally illustrated. This combination makes it easy to read, easy to digest and easy to learn from.

TEACH YOURSELF BOOKS
SHOOTING

Cogswell & Harrison Limited

TEACH YOURSELF BOOKS
HODDER & STOUGHTON
ST. PAUL'S HOUSE WARWICK LANE LONDON EC4P 4AH

First printed 1970
Second edition 1976

ISBN 0 340 203773

Printed in Great Britain for Teach Yourself Books,
Hodder & Stoughton, by Fletcher & Son Ltd, Norwich

FOREWORD

I am delighted that a book on shooting has been added to the Teach Yourself Series.

There is more opportunity each year for young people to take part in all forms of recreation and it is essential for them to take full advantage of the longer periods of leisure that we now have and which will tend to increase in the future.

Nothing is better for us than being able to share with others the enjoyment of the fresh air and our countryside. The more intense our lives become, the greater is the need for healthy recreation.

Some of us have been fortunate enough to be introduced to shooting from an early age by a father or elder brother, but there are those who are not so lucky and who would like to shoot, but do not quite know where to begin. This book which I enjoyed reading and which I warmly commend, deals with all aspects of shooting.

The chapters by Mr. Tucker on the more technical aspects are full of expert advice, are written with authority and should be studied carefully as should Mr. Turner's advice on 'Gun Safety' which should be read and re-read by the beginner. His chapters on the gun-dog and game shooting brought back many nostalgic memories and are delightfully written by a man who knows and loves the countryside.

I am sure those who read this book will enjoy every page.

Adam Block

Twinley Manor,
Whitchurch,
Hampshire.

Adam Block
May, 1969

CONTENTS

INTRODUCTION

Representing one of the world's leading gun-makers, it gives me the greatest pleasure to sponsor this book and welcome the reader into the shooting fraternity, a brotherhood without equal.

I have been fortunate to have held a gun in my hand since my boyhood days and, albeit the years are now rolling by, I still look forward to my next day in the open air with just the same enthusiasm as in those halcyon days when my lungs did not protest at any exertion and my legs supported me without complaint over the roughest ground or steepest hill!

Shooting, to me, is the finest sport there is, and the newcomer has a wealth of enjoyment to which to look forward. Not only has the enthusiastic novice a great deal to learn about the handling and control of fire-arms but, whether his addiction is shot-gun or rifle, he comes to cherish the open air and countryside into which his sport leads him, prize the knowledge which he learns from the craft and value the comradeship of the many good men he meets either in line in the field or in combat on the range.

Most of my longest and dearest friendships have risen from shooting encounters in England and abroad, and it has been my good fortune during my shooting life to witness some first-class marksmanship with all types of fire-arm, watch with fascination displays of wood and fieldcraft by experts, and myself learn something of the wile and wariness of game of all species and sizes. I can only hope that every reader of this book will, in the days ahead, be able to cherish as many memories.

In sponsoring this volume I have been fortunate to have at my disposal the knowledge of a famous and successful Bisley marksman who has contributed, in the limited space allotted to him, a fund of information for the beginner to digest. He is also an enthusiastic game shot, and he and I are members of a happy little syndicate which includes an old friend who, in a past which is farther away than we both care to remember, presented me in Bombay with my first lethal weapon, a Daisy air rifle! With a fund of varied experience, I thought it fitting to call upon him to contribute also to this book, and I should like to thank these gentlemen for their valued support.

It now only remains for me to wish every reader 'good hunting', with the hope that the contents of this book will help him over the first few stepping stones of his shooting career.

E. L. Holden,
Managing Director,
Cogswell and Harrison Limited
168, Piccadilly, London W.1.

In order to retain his amateur status A. St. G. Tucker has accepted no fees for his contributions to this book, on the advice of the British Olympic Association.

We are indebted to the late W. H. Fuller for the illustrations contained in several chapters of this book.

Maurice Turner has illustrated his own chapters and A. St. G. Tucker's chapter on Wildfowling.

THE GUN-DOG

Maurice Turner

A dog is mentioned here and there in succeeding chapters, but just a few general words on the subject of gun-dogs may not come amiss.

A well-trained dog is often worth half a line of beaters, particularly if it works thick cover, although a poorly trained or flighty dog is nothing but a nuisance and irritation to the syndicate.

The decision whether to keep a gun-dog is not to be taken lightly. If the beginner lives in a third-floor flat in a town with no amenities for exercise or training, then he should discard the idea at once. Also, it is sheer cruelty to keep a dog shut up all day if its owner lives alone and goes out to work.

A gun-dog can be not only a great asset to the novice sportsman but a delightful household pet as well, and no harm is done if it is befriended perforce during weekdays by a wife or any person with whom its owner is living, who can give it affection, regular exercise and meals. Any gun-dog is a readily adaptable creature, and it will associate its owner with the best of life if he pays it a certain amount of daily attention and gives it plenty of interesting week-end occupation.

Not long ago many considered it desirable for a gun-dog to have a stiff course of training with a game-keeper, and be kept in a kennel like a zoo animal and treated with strict severity. I do not think that a dog behaved any better in the field for such treatment, and the owner lost the eminent satisfaction of having the devotion of a life-long pal.

Nowadays the training of dogs is simplified and does not take endless time. Obedience clubs and gun-dog clubs—both look askance at each other!—have sprung up all over the country. There is no reason why the beginner-owner should not join both types of club. Obedience training sessions are arranged to suit the daily worker and need occupy him for only one hour each week, with exercises set for home tuition of about a quarter of an hour each day. Intensive training for longer periods is discouraged to start with to obviate boredom setting in.

Gun-dog clubs meet rather less frequently, but for longer periods at week-ends. Meetings are pleasant occasions in the open air when actual shooting conditions are simulated. The most promising few are sometimes invited to attend shoots.

The cost of joining such clubs is negligible, as all instruction is given by devotees, and overheads only have to be covered. The club of which my wife is secretary charges an annual membership fee of twenty-five pence, and the weekly charge for an hour's tuition is ten pence.

No club, as far as I am aware, will accept a puppy for training under six months old, but if both types of club are patronised the dog should, within twelve months, become proficient at heel-work, distance control, scenting, retrieving, sitting, lying or standing to order, jumping, swimming and working usefully in open fields or cover. During this time a dog will have become thoroughly used to noise, other dogs, and plenty of people around and remain steady under varying conditions. It should also respond to whistles.

Some owners take their dogs into the field with the

syndicate when only a year old. This I consider is on the young side, and it is asking a lot of a puppy to be completely steady in such a brief period.

For details of your nearest clubs I would recommend a line to the Secretary, The Kennel Club, 1 Clarges Street, London, W.1. He will be only too ready to help you.

And now for the selection, which is purely a matter of personal preference. The choice is virtually limited to Spaniels, Retrievers, which include Labradors, and Setters. The once very popular Cocker Spaniel, although there are still many good working dogs about, is becoming so in-bred for show purposes and shrinking to lap-dog size that its choice as a shooting dog is growing more problematical with time. Any of the Retrievers or Setters are lovely, affectionate and responsive dogs to own, but they are costly to feed, require a great deal of exercise, and are rather large for thick cover.

I favour the English Springer Spaniel, not because my wife and I have three of our own but because I consider it to be the best all-rounder of these days. It will cheerfully carry out all duties required of it when out shooting, is a most adaptable creature, and a loyal and devoted home companion. But I must not try to influence the reader, because, for one thing, puppies of any good working breed are not always immediately obtainable.

The beginner, having made up his mind, should not rush off to the nearest pet shop, but study the advertisements in one or two of the 'doggie' papers, perhaps *Our Dogs* or *Dog World,* and possibly the *Field* and *Country Life* for puppies already for sale or forthcoming litters. It is a good thing, too, to get in touch with the Secretaries of your local dog clubs, who are frequently asked to advertise available puppies, and good clubs should recommend only reputable breeders.

The reputation of breeding kennels can be ascertained only from local enquiry, but the beginner or a close friend is almost certain to be acquainted with a knowledgeable dog enthusiast who will be only too pleased to assist him in selecting his puppy. Pedigrees should, of course, be closely studied, but they should not be all-influential, as weak and badly formed puppies can sometimes be born to faultless bitches. Also, a pedigree may be most impressive yet consist of strains which have essentially been bred for show purposes only.

Enquiries should be made to ascertain if the breeder has heard of any gun-shyness in the ancestry of the litter. If hereditary gun-shyness exists, it could be very difficult to eradicate, and the dog might be a hopeless investment for shooting purposes. Do not be alarmed if your puppy, anyway, is at first rather startled by sudden noises and thunderstorms. It will soon learn that clatters and bangs are not intended to do it harm, and when once it has become used to the din of everyday life it should accept its first gun-shot without turning a hair.

Whether to select dog or bitch is a debatable point. Bitches are, perhaps, better workers and rather more receptive when under training, but there are these annoying bi-annual seasons of roughly three weeks each when your bitch is out of commission and has to be closely confined to quarters. Again, you can breed with a bitch and make a few pounds yet get only occasional stud fees for your dog. No, the choice must be left to the beginner according to his living circumstances. I dare not advise him further.

The cost? If you take possession at, say, two to three months you should procure a well-pedigreed good-looking healthy puppy for a maximum of twenty pounds. A private breeder might charge substantially less, and would be concerned not essentially with price, but also with a good home and good ownership.

When you have got your puppy remember to register it with the Kennel Club and to consult your veterinary surgeon about inoculations. Have an earnest talk with your wife, or whoever it may be, that the puppy is to

answer to only one name and must not be called, say,
'Rufus' by you and 'Squiffles' by her. Then the puppy
must respond to the same words of command when starting its babyhood training with rubber bones or balls. It
will become confused from the start if you tell it to 'fetch'
and your wife tells it to 'bring'. There must be uniformity
of command when two people are bringing up a dog
which is destined to become the valuable asset of a shooting man. One important lesson for a puppy to learn
before it begins its regular training is to give up a
retrieved article. Nothing should ever be dragged or
pulled from a puppy's mouth.

Finally, please do not inflict corporal punishment. A
puppy will very soon react to the word 'no' if shown
clearly with what it is connected. If rather stricter correc-
tive treatment is called for, then take hold of the loose
skin on either side of the neck and shake the puppy. It
will lose its dignity and remember such painless treatment far longer than a much resented beating.

So good luck to the novice sportsman if he takes the
plunge. If his dog develops along the right lines and, if
conscientiously trained there is every reason why it
should, he will have made a wonderful friend, discovered
an absorbing hobby and be the envy of his syndicate.

BEFORE SHOOTING

A. St. G. Tucker

So you are going to take up shooting. This means that you have got to make plans and come to decisions about equipment, some of which will probably be irrevocable. Some background information is therefore offered in the hope that it may help the beginner to make those plans somewhat easier to formulate.

CHOOSING YOUR WEAPON

The shot-gun. A visit to a gunsmith or gun-maker can be both interesting and confusing, educational and reward-ing. You may be shown all manner of weapons from sidelocks to boxlocks, single-barrelled to pump-actioned guns, English to Russian weapons. So how do you know what will suit you—and why?

Of primary consideration in this—as in all things—is the financial question, but try not to let this restrict your choice too rigidly. One can obtain a single-barrelled gun of foreign manufacture for under £25, or its British equivalent for under £50. Such weapons, however, are more for the shooter who is not yet sure of himself than for the shooter who knows that he will want to pass on the gun of his choice to his son. It is well worth spending a little more in order to make a lasting investment, even if this necessitates an arrangement with one's bank manager!

The Continental non-ejector is probably the next step up the financial ladder, but be careful in your choice, because there is quite a selection, and the quality varies considerably. Take care, for instance, that you make your choice from a dealer who is a member of the Gun Trade Association, for such membership will mean that the dealer has been carefully vetted and found to be completely reputable. Ensure that the dealer himself guarantees the weapon, and that he can provide after-sales service in the event of a malfunction. If you have a friend who has a working knowledge of guns who can accompany you, so much the better. The same considerations apply to the foreign-made double-barrelled ejectors, of which there is an even wider choice.

The semi-automatic and pump-actioned shot-guns which are so popular in the United States and other countries have never enjoyed the same popularity in this country. Perhaps they do not appeal to the traditionally conservative taste of the British shooter either aesthetically or mechanically. They are used more for clay pigeon, wildfowling and rough shooting than for game shooting, but are more prone to mechanical failure than the traditional side-by-side gun.

The side-by-side English gun is the best in the world, and is acknowledged as such universally. Generations of skill and craftsmanship ensure that it is the best in every way, but such perfection has to be paid for. The English gun is more expensive than the other types I have mentioned, but in the long term it is the cheapest, and the best investment. Its value will appreciate with the years provided it is well cared for, and there is many an English gun in use today that cost someone's grandfather a few pounds at the end of the last century, the value of which today is hundreds of pounds. The loving care lavished on each gun during manufacture ensures that the chance of mechanical failure is minimal, thus cutting running costs in a way that few foreign guns can boast. Therefore, although the initial purchase price will be high, it is money well spent.

There is one more type of gun that must be mentioned —the over-and-under, having one barrel on top of the other rather than traditionally side by side. In this country they are little favoured for general use, for some obscure reason, but are much in favour among clay-pigeon shooters. A few have been made, and still are made, in this country, but their prices range up to several thousand pounds. The more common are of foreign (usually Continental) manufacture and are to be found in a great variety of styles and qualities—with prices to match!

Ejector or Non-ejector

When a gun fitted with ejectors is fired and opened the fired cartridge cases are thrown clear automatically, thus making the reloading process quicker than with a non-ejector, from which it is necessary to remove the fired cases manually. Thus the ejector has an obvious advantage over the non-ejector, and because of this and a slightly more complicated mechanism, the price will be slightly higher. One never knows when it will be necessary to shoot quickly, so it is as well to be prepared.

Possibly the only case in which an ejector gun could be a positive handicap is when wildfowling in marshland. It is so easy in this type of shooting to foul the action with mud, and it is so easy to jam and damage an ejector with mud that it is often preferable to use the less-complicated non-ejector, even if it may make you a little slower.

What Bore?

I do not propose to enter at length into the endless argument that surrounds this question. I would rather merely offer a few simple pointers based on opinions formed over the years as a shooter and as a gun salesman.

The ·410—a very useful little weapon for short ranges. It has a limited killing power in view of the amount of shot in the cartridge, and will tend to frustrate the beginner because of this.

The 28-bore—a more unusual gun than the ·410, but a beautiful little weapon to handle and shoot. An ideal gun for the young beginner providing he is lucky enough to find one. Cartridges are a little difficult to find in stock in the country, but can be obtained to order.

The 20-bore—probably the most frequently used young beginner's gun. A wide variety are available new and secondhand in a wide range of prices. Also a very popular gun with the ladies.

The 16-bore—rather fallen in recent years from the popularity it once enjoyed, probably because it is so tightly sandwiched between the 12- and the 20-bore. A very useful gun nevertheless.

The 12-bore—the most widely used shot-gun in the world. Easy to use and effective at a good range. Available in all shapes and sizes, and at all prices. If you can manage it physically, choose it in preference to all others at a price to suit your own pocket.

Obviously when choosing a gun it is essential for various reasons to seek the advice of a gun-maker. If you buy your gun from a gun-maker you will get this advice anyway, but if you buy the gun privately it is even more essential that you should obtain the advice and opinion of a gun-maker. There are many guns which change hands privately that are so dangerous that no gun-maker would buy or sell them. It is all very well getting a 'bargain', but if it is more lethal to the user than to the quarry it is no bargain.

The sort of advice that a gun-maker can give you will concern the safety of the weapon, any repairs that are necessary if you are buying it privately, and whether it will suit your physique. The safety factor (apart from mechanical flaws) hinges on the nitro-proofing of the weapon. This is a test carried out on every British weapon by the London or Birmingham Proof House. Some foreign weapons are similarly tested when they reach this country, but some countries have their own proof houses, which are recognised in this country. The test involves the firing of a specially loaded cartridge which will generate a pressure approximately 65% in excess of that generated by a commercially sold cartridge. The high pressure is sufficient to show up any hidden flaws or weaknesses, and thus the test is in the form of an insurance not only for the user but also to the vendor. When a shot-gun is nitro-proofed it is marked to show the limits to which it is tested, i.e. chamber length and bore diameter. A gun-maker can quickly check the weapon with his gauges and pass an opinion, and since he will seldom charge for such advice, you have nothing to lose—but you could save a lot.

The fitting of your weapon to your particular physique is of extreme importance. Wherever you buy your gun it is essential that the stock should fit you, and the only sure way of doing this is to go to a shooting school. There are many things that are taken into account when a gun-maker fits a gun to a customer, e.g. eyesight, build, length of arm and neck, shape of face, size of hand, position of left hand on barrels and any physical peculiarities. These factors will govern the length of the stock, the bend (or 'drop') and the cast. 'Bend' is the distance between the comb of the stock and an imaginary line extending rearwards along the top rib of the barrels, and is measured at two points—the comb and the heel. 'Cast' is the distance that the stock is moved sideways to compensate for the left- or right-eyed shooter, and is measured at three points —at the comb, heel and toe. If the stock is set for a right-handed shot it is 'cast-off', and if it is set for a left-handed shot it is 'cast-on'.

Having a gun that does not fit you is like wearing someone else's suit, and your shooting will suffer. I shot for many years with no professional tuition, and shot most indifferently. Then I decided to go to a shooting school, and it was only there that I found out—in one hour—all the faults that had become ingrained over the years. I was shown how to correct them, and have enjoyed a considerably improved standard of shooting ever since, with the stock of my gun built to suit me—and me only. It is the most profitable hour's shooting with a shot-gun I have ever had. It is possible to fit a gun to its owner in the shop when making the purchase, but only approximately. Under 'field conditions' at the shooting school, however, it is much easier, because you are shooting naturally, and the instructor can then make a true assessment of your individual requirements.

Barrel Length

In the old days of black powder, at the end of the last century, 34-in. and 36-in. barrels were all the vogue, because the powder burned for the entire length of the barrel. Thus the longer your barrels, the higher the velocity of the shot when it left the muzzle, and the longer the range. With modern smokeless nitro powders the length of barrel makes no difference to the range. Over the last ten years 25-in. and 26-in. barrels have gone to the top in popularity in preference to the 28-in. and 30-in. of our fathers' day. Whereas they are hard to find secondhand, they are commonplace new. The obvious advantage is that they are considerably easier to handle and, being generally lighter, they come up to the shoulder more quickly. Try several barrel lengths if you can, for the length you will choose will be more a matter of personal preference than anything else. However, if you are slightly built your obvious choice will be a gun as light as possible, whereas if you are big and strong your choice will not necessarily be a big heavy gun. Always remember, though, that a gun which weighs $6\frac{1}{2}$ lb feels considerably heavier at the end of a hard day's walking over plough, etc.

When you have chosen your gun, whether privately or from a gun-maker, there are certain other essentials to be paid for. At the head of my list would be insurance not only for the gun but also to cover any accidental damage you may do with it to persons or livestock. Many a shooting career has been terminated abruptly, even if only temporarily, by damage to a gun which was uninsured, so it is well worth the annual premium. A gun case is also an important acquisition, since an unwrapped gun left in a corner is so easily damaged, and a cover is a good idea for ease of carrying in the field.

A comprehensive cleaning kit is a 'must' for any shooter. It is not regular use which will shorten the life of a gun but misuse, under which heading lack of proper or regular cleaning is possibly the most common factor. The kit should comprise a cleaning rod, jag, phosphor-bronze brush, wool mop, patches, a vegetable oil (for general cleaning of the gun and rust prevention), a fine mineral oil (for inside the action) and a duster. The usual oil sold for gun cleaning is an aqueous solvent, i.e. one can mix it with water to make a cleaning solution. Dip your phosphor-bronze brush in the solution (having screwed it on to your cleaning rod!) and scrub the insides of your barrels until you can feel that the outsides are warm. This will open the pores and let all the burnt powder out. Then wrap a patch round your jag and rub the insides of the bores with it until the patch comes out clean. Having done this, pour some of your cleaning oil on your mop and push it down the barrels once, leaving a thin protective film. Now that the insides of the barrels are clean, the outside of the gun (excluding the woodwork) must be cleaned of all mud, blood and water and rubbed with an oily rag, or duster, again leaving a thin protective film of oil. It is essential that you carefully oil round the triggers, trigger guard, ejectors, top lever and up the sides of the ribs—all those places which are a little awkward to clean and where the rust therefore forms quickest. It will be necessary to use the mineral oil on the action infrequently, but when it is necessary a few drops round the triggers should be sufficient. Never try to strip the action—that is what gun-makers are for! A light rub over the woodwork with linseed oil is also a good idea occasionally to keep the weather out, but be sure to remove all dirt first, especially from the chequering, with a stiff brush. Lastly, remember, when you come in after shooting, look after your gun before you look after yourself, because rust forms so very quickly.

Cartridges

With the exception of 12-bore cartridges, there is very little choice in this country apart from shot size and length. The shot size will depend upon what you are shooting, but as a general rule No. 6 shot can be used for everything except geese (BB or No. 1), duck (No. 4), snipe (No. 7 or smaller), hares (No. 4) and foxes (No. 4). The length of cartridge will depend upon the length of the chambers of your gun, but because you have—for example—$2\frac{3}{4}$-in. chambers you do not have to use $2\frac{3}{4}$-in. cartridges. You can use a standard $2\frac{1}{2}$-in. cartridge, providing you clean your chambers well after use. Obviously plastic cases are preferable to paper cases, in that they are waterproof, but some farmers object to them because the weather does not rot the fired cases and they lie around for years.

With a 12-bore you have wider range of cartridges. There are, for instance, special cartridges for trap shooting, skeet shooting and trench shooting (all types of clay-pigeon shooting). You also have a variety of loads in the standard $2\frac{1}{2}$-in. cartridge, from 1 oz, $1\frac{1}{16}$ oz and $1\frac{1}{8}$ oz, to the hard hitting $1\frac{1}{8}$ oz shot load, in which our Blagdon cartridge probably leads the field in popularity. You will find by experiment which cartridge suits you and your gun best, so do not be afraid to try a variety of them.

Naturally something to hold your cartridges is a necessity, and whereas one can use a pocket, it is not entirely to be recommended, since it will not improve the shape of the garment. Besides, if some extraneous item in the pocket should slip into the chamber in front of a hurriedly loaded cartridge the result could be disastrous. So you should rely on a belt, a bag or a dispenser. The belt is available in canvas, canvas with leather loops, leather with open-ended loops, leather with closed-ended loops or leather with metal clips, in ascending price order. The leather belt with open-ended loops is probably the most popular, since it is reasonably priced and the cartridges can be removed easily and quickly, but whichever you choose, remember that it will often be worn over a lot of clothing, so ensure that it is sufficiently long. Bags are available to hold 50, 75, 100 or 150 cartridges, and are made of canvas, hide or pigskin, once again in ascending price order. They are virtually waterproof, but if you are going to carry one around on a rough shoot do not get too large a bag, because it gets very heavy by the end of the day! The dispenser consists of a waterproof tube carried over the shoulder, with a spring-loaded release clip on the end which will release either one or two cartridges. Produced between the wars, it went out of production and was reintroduced by us in the early 1960s as a result of popular demand. The obvious advantage is that the cartridges are kept dry, and it can therefore be used in any weather without the cartridges getting wet and swelling. When it is raining you have to keep a belt under your clothing, which is very inaccessible, and if the cartridges are in a bag they get wet as soon as the flap is opened.

Clothing

Obviously one of the most important requirements of shooting clothing is that it must be waterproof as well as warm. It must also allow freedom of movement, and must be more roomy round jacket shoulders than ordinary clothing to allow the arms to swing. Bright colours should obviously be avoided, because camouflage is a necessary factor. In addition, if you intend to participate in any type of shooting which requires stealth, such as stalking or hunting, it is obviously necessary to choose clothing which is quiet.

The hat should have a wide enough brim to keep the sun out of your eyes and the rain from pouring down your neck.

The jacket should have a storm collar, preferably a storm front, ample pockets (including a breast pocket), storm cuffs and should be a good deal longer than an ordinary jacket to make a waterproof overlap over the trousers. A lining is not strictly essential, because any number of garments may be worn under it. A detachable hood is also a very good idea, as is a large inside 'poacher's' pocket, and many modern shooting jackets offer these refinements.

Trousers can be obtained to match your jacket, but if you are going to do a lot of walking through brambles, over barbed-wire fences, etc., then nylon trousers are quite useless, because they tear too easily. The really satisfactory answer is a strong pair of leggings. These also allow complete freedom of movement, a very important factor when selecting your apparel.

Footwear could occupy a chapter on its own but the important factors to remember are comfort, flexibility and waterproof qualities. Whether you have leather or rubber, ankle length or calf length is really a matter of preference, but the leather will last the longest in rough conditions, providing it is well treated and maintained.

Your gun-maker's shop will have all manner of useful and tempting items to show you, but practical experience rather than salesmanship on his part will show you what accessories will be useful to your type of shooting. However, the items which I have listed and described will help you to begin in the right way, so let me simply say at this juncture—'Welcome—to the sport of kings.'

GUN SAFETY

Maurice Turner

'All the pheasants ever bred, don't make up for one man dead.'

So ends a little ditty which I was enjoined to learn by heart before my first four-ten was put into my hands.

Nowadays, cheap shot-guns are too easily obtained by trigger-happy delinquents who have no more regard for safety regulations than for road-traffic signs. Accidents, fatal and otherwise, from carelessly handled firearms are on the increase. I could write heatedly about these, but we are more concerned with safety in the field, and I am sure that the beginner will not resent a few words of advice on this subject.

Let us then begin our little rhyme.

> *If a sportsman you would be,*
> *Listen carefully to me,*
> *Never, never, let your gun*
> *Pointed be at anyone.*
> *That it may unloaded be*
> *Matters not the least to me.*

In days gone by small boys were severely chastised if they so much as pointed a cap-pistol at near relatives! In these days parents are not so severe, although when the beginner has acquired his shot-gun he must realise that he has become the owner of a very lethal weapon, and must treat it accordingly. He is going to take it out among his fellow humans, any of whom can be fatally injured through carelessness or misappreciation.

Firstly, then, whether they are loaded or unloaded, the novice sportsman should always keep his barrels pointing downwards or skywards. When carrying his gun prior to or after action the stock can be tucked under his right arm with the fore-end resting on his forearm. Alternatively, he can carry it in the 'slope' position with trigger-guard inwards and the left hand covering the butt with palm inwards. This will ensure that the stock is well tucked in and barrel ends are well above head level. Heaven help us from the man who shoulders his gun horizontally and waves it among the faces of his colleagues! Equally to be deplored is the uncomfortably stupid habit of tucking the gun between both elbows and resting it in the small of the back!

When 'walking-up' in action the beginner's gun should be held 'at the ready'. This means that it should be carried most conveniently for raising swiftly to the shoulder, with the fore-end resting in the left hand and the right hand grasping the pistol grip of the stock, with the barrels pointing down at an angle of more than forty-five degrees. The beginner should not keep a forefinger curled round a trigger, as it is easy to jerk off a shot prematurely when the gun is being raised. Usually I carry my gun with the safety catch 'on' and automatically thumb it forward when raising my gun to my shoulder. This is a precaution to which not every sportsman will subscribe.

While waiting for driven birds the gun should be similarly held, but with the barrels pointing skywards, as the sportsman will be anticipating tall shots. He can comfortably rest the stock in his right thigh during interludes of inactivity or tuck it under his arm, whichever he prefers.

When a fence or ditch you cross
Though of time it cause a loss
From your gun your cartridge take
For the greater safety's sake.

This rule is paramount, because most shooting injuries, fatalities and suicides are caused by gun-owners falling over their own feet when crossing obstacles with loaded guns. The beginner should make it a golden rule that he unloads his gun when any circumstance arises, whether it be the circumvention of fence, ditch or hedge, which could cause him to fall or stumble and lose control of or drop his weapon. 'It's quite all right, the safety catch was on' is one of the most common excuses when a shoot's manager remonstrates because he has caught out and, quite rightly, chastened a fellow gun for being careless. Safety catches are not infallible, and can fail at the crucial moment, just as much as any other piece of mechanism.

If a kindly colleague offers to hold your gun for you while you are negotiating a fence or gate, then, at the very least, 'break' it before handing it over. If you offer assistance, break the gun ostentatiously if you have any doubt that it has not been unloaded. If you prop your weapon against a fencing-post or gate-post while you climb over—a habit I would not recommend, because it invites damage—unload it just the same. Do not, as I have often witnessed, leave it fully loaded, then reach over and haul it up with the barrel ends pointing straight at your face!

I can only emphasise once again, be very strict about unloading or breaking your gun when surmounting any obstacle, however simple the operation may seem to be.

Game can hear and game can see
Therefore still and silent be.
Don't be greedy. Better spared
Is a pheasant than one shared.

Two of these lines in our rhyme are a deviation from safety regulations, but we can adapt the other two sufficiently well so as to caution our beginner against firing at everything he considers is within his range. Remember that other members of your syndicate are entitled to their share of the shooting, so do not indulge in the habit of banging away at birds just because you are loaded with pepped-up cartridges which may reach them! Occasions must often occur when a bird rises within easy range of two or three guns. It is better that it should get clean away than be saluted by six barrels and disintegrate in mid-air!

It is good to practise courtesy when shooting and to leave the shot to whichever gun the bird obviously belongs. If he misses, you can always cough deprecatingly!

The man who is greedy is, nine times out of ten, a danger, as he will tend to fire down the line of guns. Not only that, which is bad enough in itself, but he will be a perpetual worry to his fellow sportsmen, whose eyes will rove in his direction every time a bird rises, wondering if defensive action will be called for! This creates an inevitable deterioration in marksmanship.

This may be a good point at which to introduce the serious offence of firing down the line. A novice sportsman may set out with the best of intentions, yet forget the basic safety rules through over-excitement. The most dangerous temptations to the shooting fraternity are, probably, the hare running the gauntlet and the partridge breaking back. The beginner must conquer the extremely lethal habit of forgetting everything but his shot when game is crossing the line, and continuing his swing until his aim embraces either the ankles or heads of his friends according to whether a hare or partridge is the target.

Flank guns are particularly vulnerable on these occasions and, although the flanker may seem to be well out of range, never consider it safe to fire directly at him because of intervening distance. Remember that shot-gun pellets can blind a man at a hundred and fifty yards and probably at a longer range than this with some modern cartridges. I have, fortunately for me, only once been hit, and that at nearly two hundred yards. Only a few pellets struck my knuckles, but they drew blood all the same. If those pellets had penetrated an eye I should probably have been partially blinded.

Until a novice sportsman has gained some experience I would advise him not to try a frontal shot, unless it is very high, at game breaking through the line, but to wait until the quarry has passed and shoot at it behind. While turning in preparation for his shot he should keep his barrels pointing earthwards or skywards and commence his swing on to his target when he is perfectly satisfied that he is clear of humanity! Shot-gun pellets, incidentally, often ricochet off the ground. A novice sportsman firing at a hare may think that it is a perfectly safe shot to take when crossing the line because his pellets will only bury themselves in mother earth. But no. Depending on the angle, he can easily damage the legs of his next-door neighbour from ricochetting pellets, which is another reason for the strict avoidance of shots in direct line with humans.

> *Stops and beaters lurk unseen*
> *Hidden by a leafy screen.*
> *Therefore if a bird flies low*
> *Prithee, sportsman, let him go.*

These couplets are self-explanatory. The beginner must learn that he should never take low-flying shots if there is a near background of hedgerow or coppice into which his pellets will 'ping'. It is not only stops and beaters who may lurk on the other side of a hedge but farm hands or even the farmer himself. If there are no humans there may be livestock, and nothing infuriates a farmer more than to see a prize heifer leap into the air with a charge of sixes in its rump! The syndicate and farmer do not want to become estranged, so equal care must be taken to ensure that livestock do not get damaged. Do not be deluded into thinking that a thick hedge will stop a charge of shot. Pellets, deflected by twigs, will scatter everywhere on the opposite side of a hedgerow, so, I say, err on the side of caution and treat low-flying game with every reserve.

And now just a word in season about the long-suffering beaters. If the novice sportsman is waiting for driven birds he should never shoot directly into cover at head height or below, unless he is absolutely convinced that the beaters are well beyond harm. There will very often be hares or rabbits in a beat, and pheasants sitting tight may offer low tempting shots when they rise. But beaters are just as human and vulnerable as anybody else, and no chances should be taken when they are getting near. Pheasants will often squat on the very edge of a spinney and fly when the beaters are no more than ten yards away. To indulge in wild firing then is absolutely criminal, and beaters will be the first to complain about a careless gun, and quite rightly so, if they think that their lives are in jeopardy.

When rabbits were thriving and special days set aside for the reduction of the rabbit population many hosts insisted that his guns should 'about turn' when the beaters were within range and thereafter only take shots at bobbing scuts! Obviously it is not practicable for the guns to turn their backs on pheasants' coverts at the crucial stage, but if ever rabbits thrive again sufficiently to make special shoots worth while I only hope that the 'about turn' rule will be put into practice once more.

> *You may hit or you may miss*
> *But for ever think of this.*
> *All the pheasants ever bred*
> *Don't make up for one man dead.*

And so we have come back full circle to the beginning of this chapter. But my little rhyme has omitted what, to me, is one of the cardinal safety rules. That is never, under any circumstances, should the beginner or any sportsman carry a loaded firearm into any building or car. He should, in fact, unload it immediately the shooting day is over. Even if he remembers vividly the moment when he withdrew his cartridges, he should not enter doorway or vehicle without a final check that the breach is empty. He should make this a golden rule.

There are many lesser rules about which I could write, such as keeping guns and cartridges away from childish or youthful fingers. If little Jimmy shoots his best friend it is father who is to blame if he has left his shot-gun lying about. But I do not want to preach a sermon, and can only leave it to the beginner to apply common sense when he is the owner of such a dangerous combination as a fire-arm and ammunition. It is better to err on the right side than take the slightest chance. Believe me, the beginner will not be ridiculed but heartily respected by his fellow guns if he is ultra-cautious.

FULLBORE RIFLE SHOOTING

A. St. G. Tucker

The popularity of fullbore rifle shooting has grown from a small beginning in the latter half of the nineteenth century into its present enthusiastic following throughout this country, and even farther afield.

In 1860 the National Rifle Association was formed 'to promote and encourage Marksmanship throughout the Queen's dominions in the interest of Defence and the permanence of the Volunteer and Auxiliary Forces, Navy, Military and Air', and was incorporated by Royal Charter in 1890. At the outset the competitors and members of the Association were almost exclusively Service personnel, who would arrive on the firing line to present a picturesque sight in their varied uniforms. Towards the end of the century civilian clubs began to spring up throughout the country, still comprised mostly of ex-servicemen, but the beginning had been made.

As time went on, the clubs became more and more numerous, and County Associations were formed to assist in their running within their county boundaries, but still under the parent association, the N.R.A. This is the situation at the present time, with most counties holding their own annual prize meetings and fielding their own teams at the National Meeting held every July at Bisley, the Mecca of every fullbore target shooter.

The first step for those wishing to join the ranks of the fullbore riflemen is to join a club which will cater for their needs. In post-war days, with the run down of Armed Forces in full swing, these are getting harder to find, since the fullbore ranges dotted around the country are gradually dwindling, having been labelled as 'surplus' in this advanced age. However, there are still very many clubs which include fullbore rifle shooting in their programme, and a letter to the Secretary of the N.R.A., at Bisley Camp, Brookwood, Nr. Woking, Surrey, will produce the name and address of the secretary of the nearest club.

Joining a rifle club will bring you into contact with men, and women, from all walks of life who have found a common interest in shooting. You need have no fear that you will 'lose face' on the firing point, for even the best of shooters or 'tigers', as they are popularly known in the shooting fraternity, will get bad scores at times for a variety of reasons. You will also find in nearly every club that there are people around you who are only too willing to help, although there may be others, as in every occupation, who jealously guard every secret they have ever learned as if their lives depended on it. But this minority is to be pitied rather than despised, for they are the kind who shoot only for what they can get out of it, and they are usually very bad losers.

Nearly every fullbore rifle club will have one or two club rifles that can either be borrowed or hired by those who do not possess their own, so there is usually no need to worry about being at a disadvantage when you first take up the sport. These rifles may be rather old and worn, in fact they often are, but at least by using them for a while you will be better able to judge whether you really like the sport, or whether taking it up was just a passing whim. If you then decide you really do have a genuine liking for it, then you can think about getting your own fire-arm and other equipment, for this is obviously the ultimate achievement, as you will then have a rifle which only you will use and care for.

The usual procedure with a new member of a rifle club is to accept him as a probationary member for some three months or so, although this is not statutory, and will vary from club to club. After that period the member's name will then come before the club committee for election to full membership, and providing he has not disgraced himself in some way, or has shown no keenness whatsoever, he will be elected. When the member is elected to full membership the officers of the club will then offer all the support needed to obtain a police fire-arms certificate, which is necessary if you wish to purchase your own rifle. This is a procedure which has only recently been popularly adopted, and has been applied because, to get a fire-arms certificate, the most valid reason that can be given is that the applicant wishes to use the weapon in question on an authorised range as a member of a Rifle Club. The police previously found that applicants were using this as an excuse for their weapons to be employed for all manner of things other than target shooting, and that they usually dropped out of the club as soon as they had used it as a means to an end. But this new procedure protects the interests of all the parties concerned, which is why it has grown in popularity.

For the purpose of this exercise fullbore rifle shooting can be put into two categories. The first S.R. (*a*), or Service Rifle Class (*a*) is virtually shooting under combat conditions, using neither sling nor backsight adjustable for windage, nor any of the comforts which are permissible in S.R. (*b*), or Service Rifle Class (*b*). Here one may use the services of a sling, windage adjustment on the sights, a glove and a lens and/or a filter may be used in the backsight. There is, however, a third category of match rifle, an advanced form of fullbore rifle shooting, which was never intended to be employed under Service conditions, but rather as a test bed for barrels and ammunition.

As this chapter is aimed principally at those who will join civilian rifle clubs and indulge in the civilian side of the sport, I propose to deal only with shooting under S.R. (*b*) conditions. But for those who wish to know more about the other two categories which I have mentioned in the previous paragraph a note to the Secretary of the N.R.A., whose address is at the beginning of this chapter, will solve any problems you may have.

When you first venture on to a fullbore rifle range with a civilian club you will be confronted with a target which

Fig. 1. N.R.A. 200 yd. target.
Black aiming mark
on a white background.
Centre ring—bull, 5, 5 in. diameter.
2nd ring—inner, 4, 12 in. diameter.
3rd ring—magpie, 3, 34 in. diameter.
4th ring—outer, 2, 48 in. diameter.

may be anything from 200 to 1,000 yards away, unless of course your club has its own practice range, which will be a mere 30 yards. Initially you will probably shoot at the shorter ranges, i.e. 200, 300, 500 and 600 yards. You will be shooting at a square target with a round black aiming mark in the centre of a white background. When you get closer to the target you will find that there are also a number of concentric rings drawn on it, emanating from a compass point in the centre of the bull. These are the scoring rings, with the 'bull' ring in the centre, then the 'inner', the 'magpie' and finally the 'outer'. These score 5, 4, 3, 2, respectively; in other words, the more shots you can keep in the centre of the target, the higher your score will be.

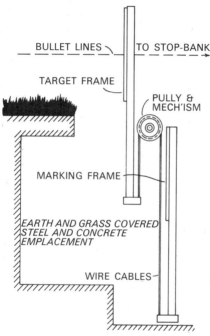

BULLET LINES **TO STOP-BANK**

TARGET FRAME

PULLY & MECH'ISM

MARKING FRAME

EARTH AND GRASS COVERED STEEL AND CONCRETE EMPLACEMENT

WIRE CABLES

Fig. 2. Arrangements at butts. The target and marker frames are balanced against each other. (Details of pulley supports and frame guides omitted for clarity.)

These targets, which are situated in the 'butts' are held in a metal frame-work which can be raised and lowered, as you will probably soon find out! To counterbalance the target there is another kind of wooden frame-work or board which goes up when the target comes down, and vice versa. This second board is usually painted white, and there is a black wooden disc which can be moved to any of the four corners of the white board to denote the hit that has just been registered.

So the procedure when one is down in the butts 'marking', or looking after the targets, is that you watch

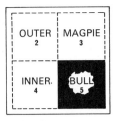

Fig. 3. Marking frame. The loose black square or disc is moved into the appropriate position.

the ground behind your particular target and when a splash of earth indicates that a bullet has hit it, having first gone through your target, you look up at the target to see the hole. Then you move the black disc on the marker board to the appropriate quarter to indicate the value of the shot. You then lower the target, thus bringing the

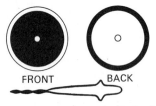

Fig. 4. Spotting disc and clip (Parker-Hale).

marker board into the view of the shooter to tell him what he has scored. Then the 'spotting disc'—a small white cardboard disc with a wire through the centre—is put in the shot-hole, so that when the target is raised the shooter will be able to see, with the aid of his telescope or binoculars, exactly where he has hit the target. This procedure is adopted after every shot has been fired, the spotting disc being moved to the new shot hole, the old shot hole being covered by pasting a coloured paper over it before the target is raised and presented to the shooter for his next shot.

This aspect of shooting 'marking' is, to many people, the most tedious and laborious part of shooting, especially if the target frames are worn or insufficiently greased, when it can be the most back-breaking task. However, there is a great deal that can be learnt from marking if one will just take the trouble. Watch, for instance, how the shots rise and fall as the light changes or how they vary from side to side as the wind varies, as denoted by the red flag on the butts. As you get more experienced you will be able to watch these points so that you can counteract them when you are shooting instead of marking.

It can be said of every sport that one can learn volumes from just watching others who are experienced, and this is especially applicable to shooting. When you first arrive at that strange mound called the 'firing point' do not be too eager to grab a rifle and start blazing away at the target at the other end of the range. Just hang around for a while, providing there are no odd jobs for you to do, and soak in the atmosphere. Watch how the experienced shooters go about the job; watch the range procedure; watch what the shooters do; and how and when they do it, for this is all valuable experience. Never be afraid to ask questions of anyone who is at hand, for the person who is keen is always welcome, besides which it is always better to ask if one is not sure, as in everything else.

When the time comes for you to handle the rifle the first thing is to feel at home with it. Explore its every angle and find out how it works and what makes it work. In all probability the rifle you will use will be either an S.M.L.E. No. 1 rifle (tried, tested and proved in the First

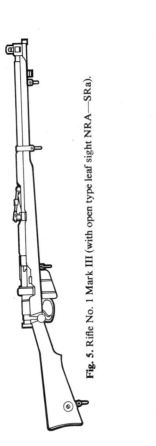

Fig. 5. Rifle No. 1 Mark III (with open type leaf sight NRA—SRa).

Fig. 6. Rifle No. 3 (Pattern 1914 or P14) Fitted with P.H. aperture rear sight.

Fig. 7. Rifle No. 4 Mark 2 (with aperture rear sight—[Parker-Hale]—NRA—SRb).

World War) the No. 3 (or P.14) or the more popular No. 4 rifle, an improved version of the former two, introduced to our armed forces during the Second World War, to their great joy and betterment!

Let us take, for the first part of our examination, the sights of this strange beast, the rifle. The foresight is a simple blade held in a block mounted on the barrel, and protected from possible damage by a metal foresight protector in the form of a 'U', with the base under the barrel and the two arms coming up, one each side of the blade, to a point above the level of the top of the blade. The backsight is in the form of an inverted 'L', with the vertical arm extending upwards from the action of the rifle on the side opposite to the bolt head, and the horizontal arm extending from the top of the vertical arm across the top of the action. The backsight aperture, the hole through which one must look to see the foresight, is underslung from the horizontal arm. One is able to change the size of the aperture to suit one's own eyesight and the conditions of light by a simple adjustment.

On the two arms of the backsight you will see vernier scales, to mark vertical and lateral adjustment. These scales are marked in minutes of angle, and are for ease of checking when it is necessary to alter the sights, to move the point of impact of the bullet on the target. It is only too easy to move the sights the wrong way in the heat of the moment, but by checking the movement on the vernier scale this mistake can be obviated.

On the vertical arm of the backsight you will find two scales, one on either side of the adjustment centrepiece of the arm, which is the case on nearly all the popular sights in use in this country. The right-hand scale is marked in hundreds of yards for easy reference, whereas the left-hand scale is a vernier and marked in minutes of angle, with a numeral marking every five minutes. Each minute, in its turn, is also subdivided, into what are called 'clicks', so named because when the knurled knobs at the extremity of each arm are turned a click is clearly audible. Depending on the model of sight in question, each minute may consist of two or four clicks. Most of the later

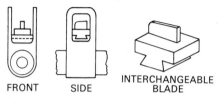

FRONT SIDE INTERCHANGEABLE BLADE

Fig. 8. Typical blade foresight and protectors on Lee-Enfield rifles.

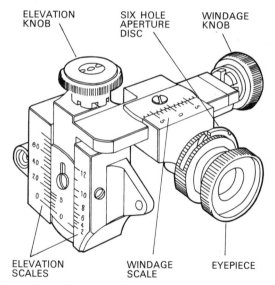

ELEVATION KNOB SIX HOLE APERTURE DISC WINDAGE KNOB

ELEVATION SCALES WINDAGE SCALE EYEPIECE

Fig. 9. Parker-Hale rear sight for the No. 4 Lee-Enfield rifle.

models have four clicks per minute, and this is a definite advantage, giving much finer adjustment.

The procedure for moving the sights is simple. If you wish to move the point of impact of the bullet on the

target over from the left towards the centre turn the
knurled knob on the lateral arm of the sight in a clockwise direction, the top away from you. To move the point
of impact upwards, turn the knurled knob governing the
vertical adjustment also in a clockwise direction. These
procedures are, of course, reversed if you wish to move
the point of impact to the left or down. Always make
sure, however, when you have made a sight change, that
the knurled locking screw holding the vertical arm is
tight, otherwise the sight may alter with the recoil of a
shot. This locking screw is there so that the backsight
arm may be detached when the rifle is not in use, so that
it will not be damaged by an accidental knock.

Also attached to the rifle is a sling, one end of which is
usually fastened just in front of the magazine and the
other halfway up the woodwork. This sling is put there
solely for your benefit, and is a definite advantage if used
correctly. If it is too tight it will restrict the circulation in
your arm, causing the blood to 'pump', which in turn will
make the rifle jump up and down. If, on the other hand, it
is too loose you will not get the proper support from it,
thus defeating the object of having it there at all. It must
be comfortable, and this is a word which is constantly
recurring in shooting as a key word, for unless you are
comfortable you cannot give shooting your full concen-
tration, and your scores will suffer. Therefore adjust the
sling so that it suits you, and if it is on a weapon which is
used by other people make a mark on it when you have
finished shooting.

At first sight, the way in which the sling is worn may
seem rather complicated, but, in fact, it is really very
simple. If you are right handed, and therefore shooting
from your right shoulder, hold the rifle in the right hand
with the muzzle pointing towards the target. Then, with
the sling hanging loosely under the rifle, put your left
hand through from left to right, and push the sling well up
your left arm nearly to the armpit. Still with the sling in

this position, bring the hand under the front of the sling and hold the rifle well up near the front sling-swivel. In this way the sling will pass from the front sling-swivel to the inside of your wrist, round your upper arm and so to the rear sling-swivel. This will give you all the support you need. One word of warning, however. The sling will usually have a buckle on it, and it is essential that this does not press against either the wrist or the upper arm, or it, too, will cause the 'pumping' previously described.

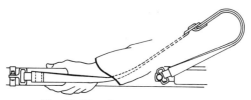

Fig. 10. Worm's eye view of sling.

If it does press against either of these points, take it off and refix it the other way round, which will usually suffice.

When you first lie down with the rifle, lay your body at an oblique angle to the target, in the way which you find most comfortable. Contrary, however, to every sergeant-major's theory, it does not matter whether your legs are splayed, together or crossed, or one is brought up to lift the hip off the ground, so long as you are comfortable (that key word again!). The way to check whether you are lying correctly is to come up to the aim, close your eyes, breathe deeply several times, open your eyes and see where the rifle is then pointing. If it is not correctly aimed, move your whole body to adjust the aim. If you do not move the whole body you will find yourself contorted, which is a source of discomfort.

Although the fullbore rifle has a definite 'kick', or recoil, this is nothing to be alarmed about, since your body will move with the kick and absorb most of it, providing the rifle is held correctly.

The left hand (presuming that you are right handed) is merely a prop, or support, and should not grip the rifle at

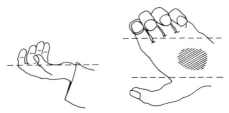

Fig. 11. The left hand. *Left-hand sketch*—looking through the side of the rifle. *Right-hand sketch*—Looking down through the rifle. The weight of the rifle should be carried at the shaded patch of the palm.

all. It should be held well forward, as far as the front sling-swivel, if you have a long arm, and it is preferable to wear a leather glove for added comfort. Positioning the hand well forward will also mean that the rifle is lower than if you were to place it, for example, just in front of

Fig. 12. The firm right-hand grip.

the magazine, and this is preferable, since the rifle will have a firmer foundation.

The right hand, holding the 'small' of the butt, with the index, or trigger-finger round the trigger, is the one which should pull the rifle into the shoulder. In addition, the chin should rest firmly against the stock, thus giving

extra steadiness. The butt of the rifle should then automatically rest in the shoulder in the correct place, since if
it is too low it will slip down when the rifle is fired,
whereas if it is too high it will force your head too far up,
giving you a crick in the neck and making it very difficult
for the eye to focus. In addition, it is preferable not to
extend it towards the big muscle on the end of the shoulder, or you will feel the kick more than you need.

When you first get on aim it is always a good idea to
fire 'dry'. 'Dry-firing' means firing the rifle without load-
ing a live round of ammunition, preferably with a dummy
cartridge or a fired case. This will give you excellent
practice in the correct way of working the trigger. The
trigger should never be 'pulled', but rather 'squeezed'.
You will find that the trigger has two pressures, or separate movements. The first pressure which is very light
(about 2 lb) should be taken when the rifle is first aimed
at the target. The second, requiring an additional pressure
of something in excess of 5 lb weight, should be taken up
when the rifle is correctly aligned on the aiming mark,
and should be a steady, controlled squeeze. You will soon
learn to judge at what stage in this final squeeze the rifle
will fire.

The aiming of the rifle is also most important. If you
are using the right eye the left eye should be either out of
focus, closed or covered with an eye-patch. When you
look through the backsight aperture the foresight blade
should be brought up from the bottom of the target to a
point just below the black aiming mark. A thin strip of
the white of the target must be left between the top of the
foresight and the bottom of the aiming mark if a blade
foresight is used. If a ring foresight is used, a ring of white
should be clearly visible between the aiming mark and
the ring round the whole of its perimeter. The reason
for this is that you have a black foresight and a black
aiming mark, so that if the strip of white is not left
between the two they will merge, and you will not know

whether the top of your foresight is aimed at the top or
bottom of the aiming mark.

The 'sight picture' (what you see when you look
through the backsight aperture) should be fairly clear,
providing you have reasonably good vision. If it is not
clear, try experimenting with the size of the aperture. If
this does not help, try to focus the eye so that the foresight is clear and the aiming mark slightly hazy. If your
vision is not too good it is no use wearing your everyday
glasses, since, when your eye looks through the sights
you will be looking through the top of the lens, giving a
bent line of vision. The remedy is, however, very simple
and inexpensive. One can obtain lenses which can be
fitted into one's backsight by means of a simple adaptor,
but as this is specialised work, it is advisable to consult
an optician especially acquainted with shooting, and the
National Rifle Association, or the National Smallbore
Rifle Association, can let you know from whom the lens
can be obtained. To those with defective vision it is in-
valuable.

You will probably know that when you hold your
breath for a long time you will eventually feel dizzy. It is
therefore obvious that if you hold your breath for very
long when you are 'in the aim', that aim will suffer. The
breath, however, must be held, but should only be held
for about five seconds. Therefore, when you have the rifle
in your shoulder and you are feeling comfortable, bring
the tip of your foresight just above the black, take up
your first pressure and breathe in. You will notice that, as
you breathe in, your foresight will drop below the target,
since the intake of breath will swell your chest, causing
your shoulder to rise, thus bringing up the butt and
dropping the foresight with your left hand as the fulcrum.
Breathe out until the lungs are about half full, bringing
the foresight up to just below the black, and hold your
breath while applying final pressure on the trigger.

If you find that you are taking too long in aim, take

your finger off the trigger, bring the rifle out of the aim and rest before coming into the aim again. Staying in the aim too long will cause the blood to 'pump' because the heart will quicken through oxygen starvation, and the rifle will jump up and down. It will also cause the sight picture to blurr and cause eye strain. Therefore, when you rest take a few deep breaths to restore proper circulation, and look at something green to relax the eyes, such as the grass in front of the firing point.

There is a maxim among target shooters that says, 'light up, sights up', and it is a very useful tip that is easily remembered. Its meaning is that when the light gets suddenly bright, such as when the sun comes from behind a cloud, the aiming mark becomes brighter in the sight picture, and its outline will not be so definite as a result of distortions. As a result, the eye will automatically allow slightly more white between the top of the foresight and the bottom of the aiming mark, although this allowance is completely subconscious. It is sometimes advisable to add a 'click' on to one's elevation on the backsight to counteract the situation, but it depends upon the keenness of one's eyesight, which only you can tell from experience.

A reasonably proficient shot will usually be able to tell where each shot has gone as soon as he has fired it, but it is when shots begin to go to unexpected places that he begins to wonder, and to try to discover reasons. Some of these are fairly easy to find, and can be 'read' from the targets, as I will now show you in the following paragraphs.

In an earlier paragraph I stressed that the left hand (in the case of a right-handed shooter) was merely a prop, and should not grip the rifle. If it does grip the rifle, albeit subconsciously, you will probably find shots going high and left of your group. This is because as soon as the rifle fires, the muscles in your left hand and arm will automatically relax due to a normal reflex. Thus the forearm will rotate upwards and to the left, using the elbow as the fulcrum, pulling the rifle with it.

Also in a previous paragraph, I mentioned that the trigger-finger should squeeze, rather than pull, the trigger. If you do inadvertently pull or jerk the trigger the shot (again in the case of a right-handed shooter) will go low

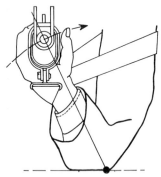

Fig. 13. Looking from the front. Gripping the stock will cause the muzzle to jump in the direction of the arrow. (Looking at the target, it will cause a high left shot.)

and to the right of the group. The reason for this is that when the trigger is jerked the whole is momentarily pulled down and to the right, this time with the toe of the butt as the fulcrum.

The reason for an unexpected high shot (apart from the foresight merging with the black aiming mark) is usually attributable to 'crawling up the rifle'. This means that the eye is brought closer to the backsight than usual, and as it gets closer the head naturally rises, until you are looking through the top of the aperture, thus raising the foresight. This is usually caused when you are on aim too long, the sight picture blurs and you crane your neck in an effort to obtain clearer definition.

The three faults which I have mentioned, probably the most common of a whole multitude, are easily corrected once they are recognised, since the cures are obvious. They do not take into account, however, the effects of wind and rain, and it is with these that I will deal now.

It will be obvious to all that wind, however slight, will affect a bullet in flight. It is probable that the range on which you will shoot will have wind flags, long, pointed flags that will show the direction and force of the wind. As a rough guide these are useful. It is possible to get scorebooks on the front of which are diagrams showing the effect of wind on these flags, varying from the flag

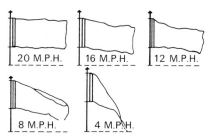

Fig. 14. Some ranges employ oblong flags, others pointed pennants.

draped down its pole for no wind to a flag at right angles to its pole for a very strong wind. Used in conjunction with this table, and incorporated in the same scorebook, are scales showing how to adjust one's sight to counteract the effect of the various forces of winds blowing from the various directions. This is all straightforward, and really needs no further explanation from me, but there are other things about the wind that demand examination.

Although I have said that wind flags are useful as a rough guide, they should never be taken as gospel. One has only to look down the range and see several flags blowing different ways to see the reason for this, besides which they may be of different weights, especially after rain. The experts' way of judging wind direction is to use 'mirage'. Mirage is caused by warm air rising from the ground, and will appear to the eye as wavy horizontal lines which will distort whatever your eye is focused on. However, even when the naked eye cannot see this mirage, it can very often be seen by using one's telescope to gain maximum advantage. The telescope should be focused just in front of the target, and the wavy lines watched carefully to see in which direction they are moving and how fast. It is amazing how infrequently the wind is constant in either force or direction for more than a few seconds.

To get really worthwhile results the telescope should be positioned in such a way that your non-sighting eye can look through it both before you come on final aim and immediately after the shot has been fired. The former will enable you to make any adjustment necessary to counteract the wind that you estimate will prevail at the time the bullet leaves the muzzle, and the latter will show you the actual wind conditions at the time of firing and will tell you how far out your point of impact should be in relation to the allowance made on the sight.

From this it may be seen that the mirage and the flags can be used in conjunction with one another. If only one is available to you at the time, then although your results may suffer, so will the results of the other shooters. But it is the shooter who can make the most of what is available to him who will have the edge over his fellow competitors.

The effect of rain on one's shooting is something that has upset many a good score, and warrants a bit of explanation. If water gets on your ammunition in the middle of a shoot you will suddenly get shots going high, so it is imperative to know the reason and the remedy.

Water on the cartridge case will act as a lubricant when the shot is fired, thus causing the case to slam back against the bolt-face faster than is normal. At every shot the barrel will whip up and down as the bullet forces its way out of the bore. When the case is dry the bullet will leave the muzzle when the barrel is at the bottom of its whip. However, when the case is wet the bullet will leave the case fractionally later than normal, by which time the barrel will be at the top of its whip, thus causing the bullet to strike higher on the target.

Once a high shot is recorded due to wet ammunition there is very little that one can do, apart from thoroughly drying the chamber and the rest of the ammunition, operations which are hardly practical in the middle of a shoot. Thus you will find it necessary to lower the back-sight by some three or four minutes to counteract the situation.

Should you find it necessary to start a competition while it is literally pouring with rain, you have a choice of two ways of conducting the shooting, 'wet' or 'dry'. This means that you can either get both ammunition and breech thoroughly wet and lower the sights accordingly, or you can cover the breech and the ammunition in an effort to keep everything completely dry. I would hasten to say here that there are two schools of thought on the subject of shooting 'wet', based on whether or not it is harmful to the rifle. I have never found any positive proof that it is harmful, and I contend that it is better to know from the outset where all the shots will go, rather than suddenly be confronted with a ruinous 'magpie' or worse, halfway through a shoot. I have always advocated and practised shooting wet. But doubtless arguments will continue on this point, and there is much to be said for and against.

To sum up, I would like to say a few words about necessary accoutrements. Obviously a telescope is most necessary, preferably one with a magnification of about 20, together with either a bipod or tripod stand. The bipod is preferable, since you can get it closer to you than a tripod, thus necessitating less movement and effort, to use it between shots. A glove or shooting mitten is also advisable, preferably the latter, to act as padding between

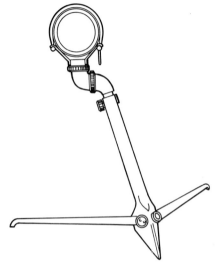

Fig. 15. Bipod telescopic stand.

Fig. 16. Shooting glove or mitt, or hand protector.

one's forward (supporting) hand and the rifle and also
between the sling and one's wrist. A proper shooting
jacket is also a definite asset, since it has padding in all
the right places (elbows, shoulder and upper arm) besides
having a gusseted back so that it is not tight across the
shoulders. Should you not wish to go to the expense of a

shooting coat, then elbow pads are a necessity for maximum comfort. A scorebook and a sharp pencil are very necessary, as is some form of 'blacking' for one's foresight to eliminate glare and reflection to obtain a clearer sight picture.

A candle will do this job, or there is a commercially produced solution sold quite cheaply in a little bottle with

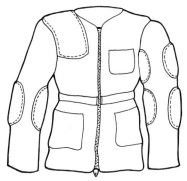

Fig. 17. Shooting coat. Padding is permitted on each elbow, round the arm carrying the sling and on the shoulder.

a suitable brush for application. A rifle rest on which to lay the rifle between shots is better than laying the rifle on the ground, and a wide-brimmed hat to keep off sun and rain is an excellent acquisition. Ear plugs are also of great value, since the 'crack' of the explosion from a fullbore rifle can be detrimental to the ear drums, as many a shooter will testify. In case of rain a waterproof pouch for the ammunition, and a cloth to cover the breech, are advisable, as is a pair of waterproof trousers and a waterproof jacket, together with a groundsheet to lie on when the grass is wet. Last and not least, it is a very good idea to have a shooting box in which to put all one's paraphernalia so that one knows where it all is, for ease of transport and to keep it dry.

Fig. 18. Rifle rest. The horns are plastic covered to save damage to the
stock.

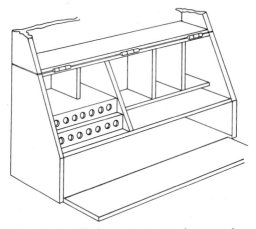

Fig. 19. Shooting box. The lower compartment houses a telescope and
stand, while the upper nests can be arranged to suit one's personal requirements.

There is nothing so exhilarating in any occupation as achieving good results, and this is especially so in shooting. But do not be discouraged if your results are not all that you would wish, for there is nothing like marksmanship to shrink a swollen head, or to boost one's ego, whichever way you look at it.

SMALLBORE RIFLE SHOOTING

A. St. G. Tucker

Quite the most infuriating question that anyone can ask a target shooter, and one that I am frequently asked, is 'What enjoyment can you possibly get out of punching holes in a piece of paper?' One might just as well belittle golf by describing it as 'an endless chase after a ball which one tries to put into the middle distance every time one catches up with it'.

Although the question is infuriating by its stupidity, it is none the less difficult to answer. Surely, however, the answer is one which covers nearly everything we do—a quest for perfection. Perfection not only in our equipment and ourselves, for these are only contributory factors, but absolute perfection in our results and our achievements. In recent years smallbore rifle shooting in the target field has become more of a precise art, a science, than a sport—a field in which perfection of equipment and self are essential to reach the top. The manufacturers of target rifles and target ammunition have really learnt from past experiences, and have produced equipment which is of scientific accuracy and design—scientific to such a degree that it is hard to imagine any further improvements, though further improvements there must surely be for the creative minds of scientist and designer are insatiable.

The parent association of smallbore target shooters in this country is the National Smallbore Rifle Association whose offices are at Codrington House, 113 Southwark Street, London, S.E.1. Although its title would suggest that it deals solely with the interests of the rifle shooter, this is not, in fact, so, for it deals with, and caters for, the ever-increasing number of pistol shooters in this country. Indeed, so rapid has been this growth in recent years that the Association's name is rapidly becoming a misnomer, as in clubs all over the country the pistol sections swell to a size which would have been a mere pipe dream a few years ago.

It is through the N.S.R.A., or through your local police station, that you will best be able to find out: (*a*) whether there is a local club which caters for the type of shooting which you require, and (*b*) the name and address of the organiser. Get in touch with him and explain what you are looking for, and he will usually be only too pleased to give you details of the club's activities. There is nothing more guaranteed to start you off on the wrong foot, however, than to adopt an attitude which quite plainly states that you consider that in joining the club you are doing the members a great honour. Target shooters are usually the most comprehensive cross-section of society imaginable, and in the main they will mix very easily, but woe betide any new recruit who considers himself a cut above the rest—even if he can score consistently high marks.

I have mentioned already that this is probably the most precise form of target shooting, but the would-be beginner should not be put off by thinking that he must 'enter the lists' with the best and most expensive equipment on the market, for this is not so. I think it is safe to say that as long as the equipment used is capable of greater things than the shooter, then there is nothing to worry about. But to spend a lot of money in the first instance when you are not even sure that you will enjoy

65

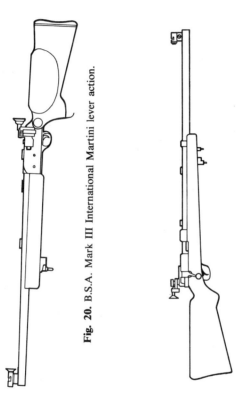

Fig. 20. B.S.A. Mark III International Martini lever action.

Fig. 21. Winchester Model 52. Bolt action.

the sport is like having your first race in the most powerful car available.

The average club will be able to supply the necessary
gear with which to start—rifle, telescope, elbow pads and
ammunition. But before you go down on the firing point
there is a lot that you can learn by merely watching the
more experienced members of the club. Watch how they
get down on to the firing point; how they wear the sling,
and position themselves; where they put the 'scope, etc.

The first thing to do is to get to know the rifle which
you are going to use—how it works, how to make it

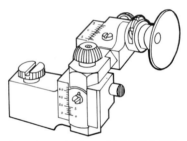

Fig. 22. Back sight. Parker-Hale model PH25C. This model is also
available in mirror image form for left-handed shooters.

work—and to feel really at home with it when you first
use it. Probably the most popular make of rifle to be
found in the club rack is the B.S.A. Martini-actioned
kind, since the variety of models which are available with
this action are so numerous as to suit every shooter. The
actions found on all these models are basically the same,
having a lever under the small of the butt which is pressed
downwards to eject the spent cartridge case and brought
upwards again to close the breech in readiness to fire. The
other type of action in which is to be found all manner of
makes and models is the bolt-actioned rifle, varying so
much in minor details that to describe them here would
occupy a whole chapter.

Familiarise yourself also with the sights, although you will not find it necessary in the initial stages to alter the backsight if you follow the generally recognised procedure which I will describe. It is sufficient at this

Fig. 23. Foresights. *Left*—Metallic element. Obtainable in many sizes. Painted, oxidised or sooted dull black. *Right*—Plastic element. The disc may be clear or tinted perspex. The black centre ring may be a countersink in the material painted dull black or a collar of black plastic.

juncture to say that one will usually have a choice of different sizes of aperture on the backsight to suit almost everyone, so do not be afraid to experiment with the various sizes until you find the one which is clearest to you. You will also see that, like some fullbore rifles, the

Fig. 24. Correct aiming.

smallbore rifle as used in civilian shooting has a round foresight in the form of a black ring. This is because the black aiming mark on the target is round, so that when you do—or should—see the aiming mark framed by the foresight ring, with a margin of white target in between the two, they do not merge. The margin of white which you should see is not a constant factor, and you will only learn by experiment how much there should be to suit your particular eye, and in order to do this it will be necessary to try various sizes of backsight and foresight apertures.

Another item of equipment which warrants examination at this stage is the sling. There are two types which may be found on a smallbore rifle—the single-point sling and the double-point sling. The former, as its name will suggest, is attached to the rifle at one end only, just under the barrel (usually on the fore-end wood) just in front of the leading—or supporting—hand. The other end is attached to the arm of the shooter, thus having the effect of steadying the weapon by pulling it back into the shoulder. The principle of the double-point sling is much the same, except that both ends are attached to the rifle, one under the fore-end and the other just in front of the trigger guard. Thus, in the case of the double-point sling, not only is the rifle forced into the shoulder but also into the side of the shooter's face. In both cases the sling should be tight enough to give maximum support without being so tight as to cause discomfort due to cramp or restriction of the blood circulation.

In the case of the single-point sling—and for the sake of convenience let us talk about right-handed shooters throughout—the other end should be attached to the upper arm as described above. The left hand should then be brought up outside the sling and on to the fore-end, so that the sling goes from the fore-end, inside your wrist and on to your upper arm. In this way the pull of the sling is directed straight from the front sling swivel to your shoulder, whereas if the sling went direct from the swivel to your arm without going inside your wrist first it would merely pull the rifle over to the left. In addition, with this type of sling you will find it advantageous to keep the left elbow farther under the rifle than with the double-point sling and the left hand as far forward as possible, thus making you adopt a low position. In this way you will get maximum benefit from the sling.

The double-point sling—the one usually used by the beginner—may at first sight look complicated, but in fact this is not so. Hold the rifle in the right hand, with the

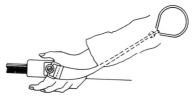

Fig. 25. Single-point sling (Worm's eye view). Detail omitted.

sling hanging down, and pass the left hand through from left to right. Then bring the left hand down under the sling and up on to the fore-end. Thus the sling goes from the rear sling swivel round the upper arm, inside the left wrist and so to the front sling swivel. Then, when you adopt the firing position, you will almost certainly find it

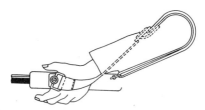

Fig. 26. The two-point sling (Worm's eye view).

necessary to adjust the length of the sling to suit you, so that you will get maximum support from it.

Most target rifles are fitted with a 'hand-stop', even if this has been fitted after manufacture, and this plays a very important part in the comfort and correct positioning of shooting. The front sling swivel is often incorporated in the hand-stop, or is sometimes positioned farther towards the front of the fore-end. It is essential that the hand-stop should be positioned correctly to suit your length of arm, and the position which you adopt,

Fig. 27. Hand stop. Below level view. The dotted portion of the adjusting bar is buried in the stock.

and to this end it is usually adjustable backwards and forwards. The secret is to position it so that you neither have to reach forward unnaturally nor are you forced to bring your hand so far back that you take too high a position. In the first case you are merely nullifying the

Fig. 28. Shooting glove or mitt, or hand protector.

support of the sling, and in the second you will find that you have too cramped a position for comfort (a key word in target shooting). Therefore, adjust it so that the left hand fits snugly against it, and it will add to the 'firm foundation' that you are building up.

As a further aid to comfort, you will find that all the top-class shooters wear a glove—or mitten—on their left hand. This is because the most accurate target rifles weigh 14 lb or more, thus making some form of padding a necessity. It is therefore advisable to get accustomed to wearing one from the outset, even though the rifle which you will use, at first, will be considerably lighter than 14 lb. The most usual type to wear is a mitten, with or without separate fingers, specially designed for the purpose.

Fig. 29. Shooting coat. Padding is permitted on each elbow, round the arm carrying the sling and on the shoulder.

Also designed for added comfort is a shooting jacket, specially padded on the shoulder, elbows and where the sling encircles the upper arm. Although it is not essential to have one of these at the outset, you should at least have some padding on the elbows, both to prevent sore elbows and to stop the elbows from slipping. Such equipment, in the form of specially designed elbow pads, is readily and cheaply available, and the small cost is well worthwhile.

Most clubs will be able to supply a telescope and stand, so that you can see where your shots are going, although this will not be necessary initially. However, if you wish to have your own, the telescope should have a magnification of 20 to 25, with fairly large light-

Fig. 30. Elbow pad.

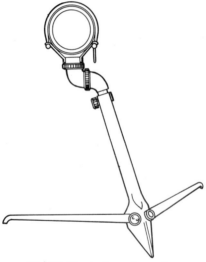

Fig. 31. Bipod telescopic stand.

gathering properties, and preferably with a screw focus. The stand should be a bipod rather than a tripod, so that it can be positioned close to you without getting in the way, thus allowing minimum movement of the head in order to 'spot' each shot.

Thus with a fairly good grounding in the theory the time is ripe to turn theory into practice. Kneel on your firing point and put the sling in position, then lie down holding the rifle in your left hand with the butt on the ground. Make a final adjustment to ensure the sling is well up the upper arm, and raise the butt into the shoulder.

It is most necessary that the position that you adopt should be natural and comfortable. Position the legs apart with the toes pointing outward, so that your body is at an oblique angle to the target. (Although you may vary the position of the legs at a later date, this is a good position with which to start.) When you think that everything is correct, sight the rifle on the target, relax and breathe naturally. Then open your eyes again, see where the rifle is aimed and adjust your whole body accordingly, repeating the procedure until the rifle is in the same position when you open your eyes as when you closed them. In order to get maximum comfort, it may be necessary to make adjustments to sling, hand-stop and length of butt, and in this one of the more experienced club members will probably be only too pleased to assist.

Having got your correct position, cock and fire the rifle to get used to the feel of the trigger and the look of the 'sight-picture'. The trigger finger should gently squeeze the trigger, and should on no account jerk, or 'snatch' it, since this will disturb the aim at the moment of firing. The other (supporting) hand should act as a rest, with the fingers well away from the rifle, since, if it does grip the rifle, that grip will automatically relax at the moment of firing, again disturbing the aim.

The positioning of the telescope has already been mentioned, but the positioning of the cartridges is just as important. Some rifles have a cartridge block attached to them for maximum accessibility, but if you use a separate cartridge block—or merely the box itself—it should be positioned in such a way that the hand can drop on it

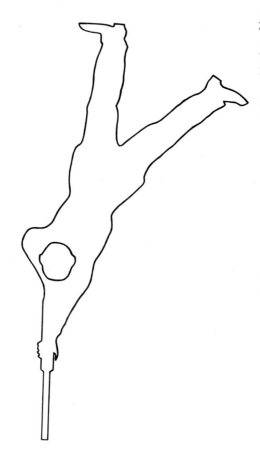

Fig. 32. The prone position. Outline sketch showing average angle of body and the positioning of legs and feet.

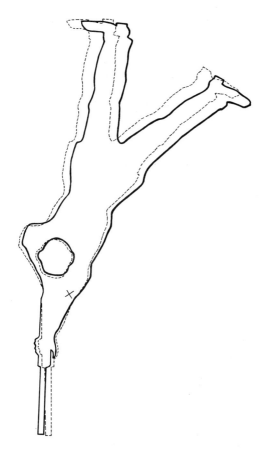

Fig. 33. It is not sufficient to swing the rifle on to the target. The whole body must act as a gun turret, pivoting on the left elbow (at 'x').

automatically, rather than your having to reach for it and disturb your careful body positioning.

When you are ready to take your final aim, breathe in deeply and you will note that the foresight dips below the

Fig. 34. The left hand. Fingers and thumb clear of the stock.

level of the intended aim. Then, as you breathe out, the foresight will lift until it reaches the desired point, when the breath should be held before the lungs are emptied.

The ideal aiming time, i.e. when sights and target are finally aligned, does not exceed five seconds. The longer

FORESIGHT RING

AIMING MARK

BREATH OUT

BREATH IN

Fig. 35. Controlling elevation by breathing.

you are on aim, the more your blood will 'pump', with detrimental results to vision and steadiness. During this time pressure on the trigger should be steadily increased until the action is triggered off. No effort should be made to pull—'snatch'—the trigger to benefit from what you think is a perfect aim, as the whole rifle will be moved by such an attempt.

As regards the procedure between shots, there are two schools of thought. I have always used a Martini-actioned rifle, and have maintained my position until the last shot, keeping the butt in the shoulder between shots. There are many, however, mostly using bolt-actioned rifles, who drop the butt out of the shoulder between shots. With this procedure it is most important that the butt is returned to the same position in the shoulder every time, thus enabling you to adopt exactly the same position for each shot. To do this, place the thumb of the

Fig. 36. Lifting the butt into the shoulder.

right hand under the toe of the butt as it rests on the ground, lever it up into the shoulder, and with practice you will find that it automatically falls into the same position every time.

You will probably find, as every beginner does, that your first few targets will have holes all over them as a result of your concentrated labours. But do not be discouraged, you are treading new ground, and making demands on your body and faculties which are completely foreign to them.

Your first step is to try to get all your shots in the black of the aiming mark. Initially, you should concentrate on one aiming mark on the target. Until you have mastered the rudiments of target shooting, and can get all your shots in a fairly tight group, it is futile to try to go round all the aiming marks on the target. In this way you will be able to see at a glance the progress which you are making and, what is more important, shooters more experienced than you will be able to diagnose your faults and help you to correct them. The initial stages are probably the most important in your career, for bad habits must be diagnosed and corrected before they become ingrained, and you will find that 'practice makes perfect' is no idle maxim—it is indisputable fact.

Fig. 37. Shots out at 4 o'clock due to snatching or pulling on the trigger.

As I have already said, the results of your first efforts may seem discouraging, but do not let yourself be discouraged. You have embarked on an endless quest for perfection—endless because it will never reach absolute perfection. You will see that with practice your groups will get tighter, and you should keep your shot targets so that you can prove this to yourself in moments of despair. As your groups do become smaller, you should watch for any tendency for odd shots to appear outside that group, for it is by diagnosing the reasons for these 'fliers' that the groups will continue to become smaller, so let us examine some of the more common faults.

Probably the commonest form of 'flier' is the one that drops out of the group low and to the right. This is usually caused by forgetting one of the rudimentary rules,

that of giving the trigger a gentle—and controlled—
squeeze, rather than jerking it. With a trigger pressure of
as little as 500 grammes there should be no need to jerk
it. If you are on aim too long (the ideal aim is one lasting
about five seconds) there is a tendency for one's co-
ordination to falter, so that although you may think that
your finger is exerting the required pressure, in fact it is
'paralysed'. Then out of sheer frustration you will tend to
jerk the trigger. So remember—a short time on aim and a
controlled squeezing of the trigger.

It should also be remembered that if you hold your
breath for very long the lungs are starved of oxygen, and
in the chain of events which follows your eyesight will
become blurred. Therefore, when this happens while you
are on aim your eye will naturally seek a clearer image,

Fig. 38. Shots out at 12–1 o'clock due to raising the head and looking
through to top of the sight.

and to do this your head will rise almost imperceptibly
until the eye is closer to the rear sight, and is looking
through the top of the aperture. This will mean that the
foresight must rise accordingly, thus raising the muzzle,
so that the resultant shot will strike high.

Another common 'flier' is the one that is high and left,
and for the cause one must look to the supporting hand.
If this hand grips the fore-end instead of merely acting as
a support it will relax immediately the cartridge ignites

due to a conditioned reflex. This will cause the muzzle to swing up and to the left, with the elbow as a pivot. Therefore, it must be remembered that the forward hand is there as a support only, and should not be allowed to hold the rifle at all.

Fig. 39. Shots out at 11 o'clock due to gripping the stock with the left hand.

Always make sure that the rifle you are using is completely in order before you begin firing. Do an organised check of the whole weapon from one end to the other in the following fashion:

1. Check that the butt plate is tight.
2. Check that the butt is not loose on the action.
3. Check that the backsight aperture is central.
4. Check that the backsight bell is screwed right home, and that the aperture is clear of obstruction.
5. Check that the backsight, and its mount, are tight.
6. Check that the nut locking the detachable arm of the backsight is fully locking.
7. Check that the foresight and foresight block have no play in them.
8. Check all other screws to see that they are tight.

Any one of the above could cause irregular and erratic shooting, and finding out the cause when the damage has

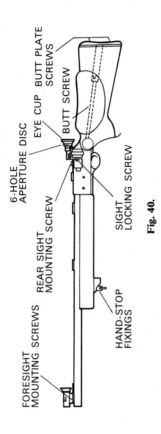

6-HOLE APERTURE DISC

EYE CUP BUTT PLATE SCREWS

BUTT SCREW

REAR SIGHT MOUNTING SCREW

SIGHT LOCKING SCREW

FORESIGHT MOUNTING SCREWS

HAND-STOP FIXINGS

Fig. 40.

been done is useless. Post-mortems are no use when the results are on the target, it is ante-natal treatment that is required.

These are only a few of the faults and their cures, for to enumerate them all would take another book, but at least these are some guide. Perhaps one other that should be mentioned is 'canting' the rifle. This means that the sights are not vertically above the line of the bore, and unless this cant is constant your shooting will suffer. Obviously it is easier, and far more natural, to keep the sights vertically above the line of the bore than it is to maintain a constant angle of cant, so keep an eye on this and ensure that the rifle is always at the correct angle.

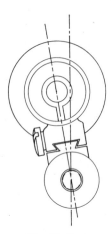

Fig. 41. Cant.

As your shooting improves and your confidence grows, you will begin to visit other ranges—be it Bisley or another local club. Here you will find that you have to contend with different conditions as regards angle of firing point, lighting, etc., etc. This is another test of one's ability, for any shooter can score well on his home range given time, but maintaining one's average on 'foreign' ground is not the same at all. But this is just another rung in the ladder on the way to club, county and national honours, and there is no fast way up the ladder, with opposition on every rung. But keep going up, for up there somewhere you may find that perfection which we all seek.

TARGET PISTOL SHOOTING

A. St. G. Tucker

Ever since the American 'Western' hit Britain with its full impact in the late 1950s, pistol shooting has increased in popularity out of all recognition as compared with the meagre collection of pistol shooters that existed previously. A pistol holds for some people a sort of magic that no other weapon does—the feeling of power that you possess when you hold one. This 'cowboy' element is latent in the majority of us, and can lead to very dangerous situations if it is not kept under very rigid control.

And so, with this recent surge of interest, and the consequent boom which has been experienced by target shooting clubs all over the country, have come problems which have not been so prevalent in the past. Men—and women—have joined their local club with some very misguided, pre-conceived ideas, and I never cease to be amused by the looks of surprise on the faces of some of these aspirants when they find that to hit a target twenty yards distant is not nearly as easy as the TV cowboys would have one believe. No less surprising to them is the fact that a 'six-shooter' really does only hold six cartridges!

The degree of safety necessary in the handling of a pistol needs to be far greater than with a rifle, simply because a slight movement of the hand which is holding it can cause the muzzle to sweep a large arc, due to the compact nature of the weapon. The weapon must always be treated with the utmost respect, if only for the peace of mind of those around.

As a rule, the first pistol you will be allowed to handle in any club will be a smallbore (·22) weapon, and in order to ascertain whether there is a club in your area you should contact either the local police or the National Smallbore Rifle Association, the parent Association of all smallbore shooters—either rifle or pistol. A letter to the Secretary at Codrington House, 113 Southwark Street, London, S.E.1, will find the name and address of the Secretary of your local club.

The choice of smallbore target pistols is wide and varied, consisting of single-shot weapons, revolvers and semi-automatics, but you will usually find that the club which you join has one or two 'club pistols' kept for the benefit of beginners who do not yet possess their own. Should you wish to purchase one of your own, you will generally have to serve a probationary period with the club before being elected a full member, and at this time you will have the backing of the club behind you to support your application to the police for a firearms certificate. This probationary period is a time wherein you will be called upon to prove by your keenness and regular attendance that you have a genuine desire to become a target shooter, and are not just using your membership as an excuse to obtain a firearms certificate to acquire a weapon for some other purpose.

When you first join a club, as with every other form of target shooting, a very great deal can be learnt by merely watching the more experienced shooters. Watch how they stand, hold the weapon, aim, etc. You will see all manner of different methods, but all stem from the basic rules and have been adapted to suit the individual.

Naturally the first thing to do is to study the safety rules which apply, by means of notices posted in promi-

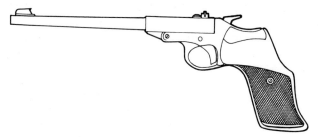

Fig. 42. Webley Mark III. Single-shot target pistol.

Fig. 43. Smith & Wesson K22 Masterpiece/Model 17.

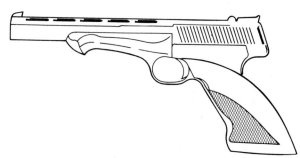

Fig. 44. Browning Medalist Pistol.

nent positions, by talking to other members and by merely watching what goes on. Most of the rules are just sound common sense (such as applying the safety catch, opening the breech or swinging the cylinder open when you are carrying the weapon), but beware that familiarity does not breed contempt.

The single-shot Webley and Scott pistol is probably the most popular pistol in most clubs for the beginner, since it is the most basic of all the pistols. It is a weapon which has been in existence—with various improvements —for a great many years, and is very simple in construction and design, yet highly accurate, comfortable to use and ever popular. By merely pressing the trigger guard down, the weapon is opened, the empty case ejected and it is ready for the next round to be inserted. Bringing the barrel upward, the breech closes, and as soon as the hammer is cocked the weapon is ready to fire. The final version has a nicely tapered barrel, a trigger which is adjustable as to the pressure needed to operate it and large moulded grips to fill the hand. These features, together with a rearsight which is adjustable laterally and vertically to suit the individual, and an attractively low price, combine to make this a most practical weapon for the beginner, and although now obsolete, it can still be obtained secondhand.

When you are first shown on to the firing point you will find that you stand behind a table on which you can put your equipment, such as ammunition, telescope, etc. These should not just be placed anywhere, but in their logical positions. Place the telescope so that you will be able to inspect the target after each shot with the minimum of effort, and *without moving your feet*. Put your cartridges down so that you can reach them with your left hand (if you are a right-handed shooter) so that you will not have to disturb your grip on the pistol when you reload. Also, do not make the mistake of trying to lean on the table for support while you are shooting. You may think that such a support would be an advantage, but besides being an infringement of the rules it will affect the flow of blood, and you will feel the blood 'pumping', and this 'pumping' will be transmitted up the body, causing your hand to move.

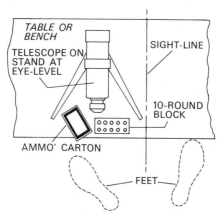

Fig. 45. Handy arrangement of equipment.

The first thing to get right is how you should stand—your 'stance'. Obviously if you face the target, stand square to it and raise your arm there will be a tendency to rock backwards and forwards. Similarly, if you go to the other extreme, and stand so that your shoulders and extended arm are in a line with the target, there will be a tendency to sway from side to side. Thus the ideal stance is halfway between the two extremes, where your feet are at an angle of about 45° to the target. You will, however, see people shooting using the two extremes I have mentioned, as anything is possible with practice and adaptation, so one cannot label these extremes 'wrong'. It is merely inadvisable to start off with a disadvantage.

When you think you are correctly and comfortably positioned look at the target and point at it with your trigger finger, in the same way that you would aim your pistol. Then rest your hand on the bench, look away and point at the target without looking at it. Then look to see where you are pointing. If you are pointing to the left, then move your right foot in an arc to the right. If you are pointing to the right, then move the left foot to the left.

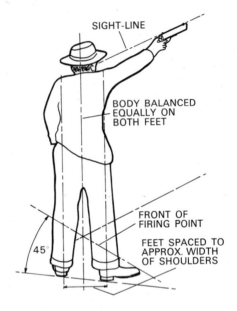

Fig. 46. Pistol stance.

Then repeat the experiment until you find you have the correct aim.

The way a pistol is held is also of the utmost importance, and should be studied carefully. The mistake which most beginners make is to hold the weapon too tightly. Their reasoning is that the tighter it is held, the less it will wobble. In actual fact, however, the reverse is the case. Thus the untutored beginner will hold tightly,

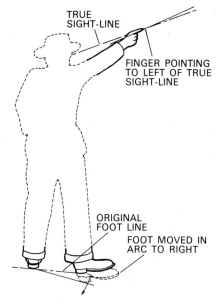

Fig. 47. Checking and correcting. Aim and foot position.

Fig. 48. Pistol grip.

see that the pistol wobbles and tighten his hold still further, until every part of his body is tied into knots and the
pistol is waving about on the end of his arm like a mad
thing! The correct hold, and the correct stance, is one
that is completely relaxed and free from all tension, thus
giving 'comfort'—a word which should be written in red
on every beginner's target.

The tips of the fingers on the hand holding the pistol
need not actually be in contact with the butt at all. The

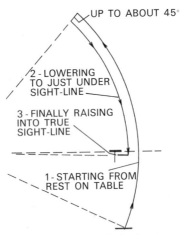

Fig. 49. Diagram sketch of hand and pistol movements on coming
into the aim.

principal areas of contact should be the base of the fingers
and the heel of the hand round the base of the thumb,
with the palm of the hand acting as a liaison between the
two, and the thumb exerting a steadying influence on the
other side of the butt. The trigger finger should exert
pressure on the trigger by means of the middle joint for
maximum control.

Relaxation of the shoulders is no less important, and I
have found that this can best be achieved by placing the

free hand in the trouser pocket, rather than hanging freely at the side (which tends to pull the shoulder down) or resting on the hip (which tends to push the shoulder up). Having done this, I raise the pistol to an angle of about 45° to the horizontal, lower it to fractionally below my point of aim and raise it just a fraction to bring it actually on aim. I am convinced that bringing it straight up from the 'rest' position to the 'on-aim' position creates maximum tension, whereas the other method merely 'locks' the aim or, at worst, creates the minimum tension.

As the arm is brought up above the horizontal, breathe in, and then breathe out as you lower the arm, holding your breath as you come on aim. The lungs should not be completely drained, however, or the heart will begin to 'pump'.

Having brought the pistol on aim, one must know how to aim and what to aim at. Aiming should be done with the right eye if you are right-handed, since aiming with the left eye would necessitate bringing the arm across the body and bending the wrist to an unnatural position to line up the sights. This does not mean that the other eye should be screwed up, because so doing would tend to reduce vision in the sighting eye. Some people wear a patch over the non-sighting eye, but most will half close it to put it 'out of focus'.

It is naturally impossible for the human eye to focus on three points as far apart from each other as backsight, foresight and aiming mark, all at the same time, and anyone who tried to prove otherwise would simply be wasting his time. It is thus recommended that the eye should concentrate on the sights, and not try to clearly define the black aiming mark as well. The most popular size of foresight is $\frac{1}{8}$ in. broad, but whatever the width of the foresight, the backsight should be sufficiently wide to leave a clearly defined strip of white on either side of the foresight when the weapon is on aim. If this is not so, foresight and backsight will merge into one, and the resultant shot could hit anywhere.

Anyone who can point to an exact spot on the target and say that he aims exactly at that spot every time he

Fig. 50. Front and backsight clearances.

fires is fooling no one but himself. It is a physical impossibility, and his scores will prove it, for if he did as he says he would never drop a point, provided his sights were correctly set. It is, however, essential to endeavour to align one's sights with an *area* on the target, and it will

Fig. 51. White gap (regulation) between sights and aiming mark.

depend upon your skill as to how large that area is. The area that you choose can be one of two—the centre of the black aiming mark or just below the aiming mark. With the former there is always a tendency to lose your sights, as they may merge into the black, especially if one is on aim too long and the eye tires. Thus it is that the latter is the choice of most shooters, since it makes for ease of maintaining a clear sight picture. With this method it is possible to leave a strip of white between the top of the foresight and the bottom of the aiming mark, so that the sights will not merge with the aiming mark.

When you first shoot with a pistol you will find it hard enough to keep all your shots on the target, let alone within the aiming mark. But this is nothing to worry about. You are using muscles which you do not use in everyday life, and until these muscles are strengthened by practice your shots will be scattered. Do not worry,

ADJUSTABLE
IRIS TYPE
APERTURE

RUBBER
SUCTION
CUP

Fig. 52. 'Pistol-Aid'. (Every part is finished dull black.)

either, if you cannot seem to keep the sights reasonably aligned on the target. The more you strive to keep them still, the more they will jump about, and the longer you are on aim the worse will become your sight picture, until everything finally disappears in a grey haze. Concentrate on a short aim with a controlled squeezing of the trigger. If you want to prove to yourself that all these things are true, turn the target the wrong way round and shoot at the back of it, and you will be amazed at the result.

If you are shooting on an indoor range under artificial lighting you will probably find that you will get a sight picture that is far from distinct, due to the brilliance of the light. To overcome this difficulty it is an excellent idea to use an 'Iris Pistolaid', a gadget made specially for the purpose and easily obtainable from the N.S.R.A. or local gunsmith. The gadget in question merely takes the form of an adjustable aperture which can be attached by means of a rubber suction cup to a pair of glasses (preferably the yellow 'sun visor' type) and cuts down the amount of light reaching the eye. The aperture opens and closes to suit individual requirements on the same principle as a camera shutter. The small outlay involved is well worthwhile, as you will find that by adjustment the sights can be brought into sharp relief.

There is often a tendency among beginners to rush through their shooting much too quickly. They somehow get the idea that they must hurry on to the next shot, which is sure to be a better shot than its predecessor. But invariably it is worse than its predecessor, and so they rush on to the next—with the inevitable result. Try, instead, to shoot with an experienced shooter, taking the timing from him, and bringing your pistol up as he brings his down, so that you will not distract each other. In between shots, rest your pistol hand on the bench, without disturbing your grip, except to take your finger off the trigger, and breathe deeply to restore the heartbeat to normal after the strain put on it by holding your breath.

As soon as your groups begin to get smaller, you can begin to diagnose obvious faults by the results on the target, and correct accordingly. One of the most common is the occasional shot high and right, and this can usually be attributed to jerking—or 'pulling'—the trigger, instead of giving it that controlled squeeze. Causes of this can be anxiety to get the shot off at the exact moment at which the sights are aligned correctly with the target; trying to get the shot off too quickly; or staying on aim for too long and getting the shot away in sheer desperation as the picture fades into a haze. The remedies for the latter two are obvious, but for the former it must simply

Fig. 53. Results of a trigger pulling with a pistol.

be borne in mind that sight alignment is merely one of several important factors to watch, but none of these factors must be concentrated on at the expense of another.

Another is the occasional shot out to the right or left of the group. This is very often caused by a backsight aperture which is too narrow, thus not allowing that important strip of white between the edges of the foresight and the edges of the backsight. Thus, as soon as the eye tires a little, it is not noticed that the two sights have merged into one on one side and, although you may not realise it,

Fig. 54. Results of using too narrow a backsight.

the weapon is pointing to one side of the usual aiming area. The remedy here is obvious—widen the backsight aperture slightly. But be careful not to leave the bare metal showing, or that, too, will affect the sight picture.

SHOT TO RIGHT   SHOT TO LEFT

Fig. 55. Effects of too wide a foresight or too narrow a backsight not allowing a clear picture of both sights.

Either apply a chemical black or hold it over a candle flame until it is covered by a carbon deposit—this being a temporary measure until you are sure that you have widened it enough. As soon as you are sure that it is the

Fig. 56. Results of too heavy a gun for the beginner or dallying in the aim for too long.

correct width, apply the final chemical black—either yourself or by taking it to a gunsmith.

The odd shot below the group can usually be attributed to one of two factors. The first is that the gun is too heavy for you, and this is something the beginner is liable to find if he starts immediately with a heavy target pistol. The untutored muscles cannot hold up the weight of the weapon and the muzzle begins to droop, and although the shooter can see this happening, his muscles may be powerless to stop it. It is something that will be overcome naturally as the muscles become stronger, but exercises to strengthen the wrist (such as opening and clenching the fist on some handy object) can speed up the process. The second cause can often be attributed to staying at the aim for too long. The eye tires, and the black of the aiming mark fades into oblivion. As it fades the eye tends to seek it to obtain more clarity, and so the foresight is put out of focus. Reacting to this, the eye tries to do the impossible, i.e. to focus on foresight and aiming mark at the same time. Result—the foresight is seen with a shadow, or ghost, sight on top of it, and the natural tendency is to take the 'ghost' sight as the correct one with which to aim. Too long on aim cannot help but be detrimental: try a rapid ten shots on a practice card, and you will be amazed at the results achieved.

A word about changing the sights. If the sights are non-adjustable—'fixed'—then the foresight will have to be reduced in height if the shots are going low, and the right-hand edge of the backsight cut back if the shots are going left—and vice versa. If the backsight is adjustable, then it must be brought into the error, i.e. up if the shots are going high, and right if the shots are going right—and vice versa.

One last word of warning. To the untutored eye pistol shooting looks easy, but many a beginner has been put off by his initial results when he finds that the opposite is the case. But do not be dismayed—the secret lies in practice, practice and more PRACTICE.

GROUND SHOOTING

A. St. G. Tucker

Thinking of the term 'ground shooting' puts me in mind of the supposedly true story of a member of the French nobility who was taking part in an organised pheasant shoot in England. His host, watching to see that all was well with his guest, perceived to his horror that he was taking careful aim at a hen pheasant which was running through the undergrowth just in front of him. Overcome with the Englishman's sense of sportsmanship, he cried out, 'Don't shoot that bird while she's running!' to which came the reply 'I do not intend to—I'm waiting until she stops!'

But seriously—there are times when it is necessary to shoot at a sitting target, usually when one is shooting vermin, and it is amazing how many people just cannot hit anything which is stationary when using a shot-gun. What they do not realise is that they must allow for the trajectory—or curved path of flight—of the shot between the muzzle of the gun and the target. Naturally, since the top of the action (which is used as a backsight when taking an aimed shot) is higher than the foresight bead, when the shot initially leaves the muzzle it will travel in a path which will take it above the line of sight. From this, it is obvious that when a shot is taken at really point-blank range the point of aim must be under the target if a kill is to be made. An old maxim that is well worth remembering is 'when you shoot a sitting pigeon, shoot at his legs', and this is very good advice for a close-

Fig. 57. Missing over at close range.

range shot. The farther away the target is, however, the higher one's point of aim must be, until it is above the target.

There can be no hard-and-fast rule about exactly

where to aim for a sitting shot, because there are many factors to be taken into consideration, such as size of shot, angle of shot, type of cartridge, etc. For a rule of thumb, however, take some of your favourite cartridges in your most commonly used shot size and lay an object on the ground, preferably hard ground, on which you can see the marks of the shot. Then pace off various distances and take a 'pot-shot' at the object and examine where the pellets have struck. You will soon learn from this how to take what is supposed to be 'the easiest shot in the book', and thus save yourself a great deal of embarrassment and 'ribbing' in the future. If you are going to take a pot-shot at a sitting target, however, the easiest way is to treat it as you would any other shot, and not 'aim' at all. Merely 'point' the gun in the normal way, and you will be amazed at the result.

Probably the two most popular ground game in this country are hares and rabbits, so let us now take these in turn. The former, being 'game', is not considered fair game for a sitting shot.

Over recent years the number of hares in this country has increased to phenomenal proportions compared with pre-myxomatosis days. A contributory factor is that until their numbers were decimated by myxomatosis the rabbits used to kill off the young hares—leverets. Accordingly, they have become a very popular game for the shooter, especially as there is no close season for killing them.

To the average rough shooter, who has a few acres of ground over which he may walk with his gun, they are usually something of a 'surprise packet'. They will lie in most exposed places, whether it is plough or grassland, and will also be found in the woods and hedges—especially during wet weather. Walking around on my own, I have often been caught completely off my guard when the ground under my feet has suddenly erupted and galloped away at speed with ears flat and tail bobbing!

Apart from the initial shock of being confronted with such an unexpected target, it is amazing how easy it is to miss a hare—as I have proved to my shame and embarrassment—simply because it is such a large target that one tends to aim at it rather than give it the lead which is so essential. Besides this, a hare can carry a lot of shot quite a distance, so that to avoid wounding it and allowing it to escape to die, use a fairly large size of shot—No. 4 is recommended.

Lead, as with every other kind of shot at a moving target, is directly proportional to the speed of the animal and the direction in which it is going. As far as the rough shooter is concerned, the usual chance at a hare will be a 'going away' shot, since the animal will probably be 'walked up'. Naturally, if the hare is running on flat ground, or along a furrow or ditch, it will be travelling faster than it would on rough ground or running across the furrows of a ploughed field. This must naturally be taken into account when the shot is taken. The correct

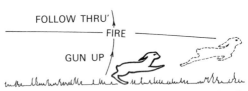

Fig. 58. (Side view of going-away shot.) Shoot to miss ahead.

way to take the shot—in fact, the only way—is to bring the gun up behind the hare, pass through the length of his body, past his head and shoot over his head. If at first you merely hit his back legs, which will admittedly bring him down if the legs are broken—to the accompaniment of spine-chilling screams and a lot of blood—keep increasing the lead for subsequent shots until a clean kill through the head is accomplished. If you find this difficult to achieve, and you keep hitting his hind legs, try to miss him in front—you will find it almost impossible, since you will hit him in the head nearly every time.

With the crossing shot the procedure is virtually the same. Bring the gun up behind the animal, swing through the length of his body and shoot in front of him. But remember—do not be deceived by his size or apparent lack of speed—the hare travels a lot faster than one thinks when watching it. As with everything else—never shoot at it, shoot at where it is going.

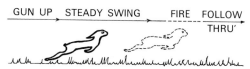

GUN UP   STEADY SWING   FIRE   FOLLOW
                                  THRU'

Fig. 59. (Front view of crossing shot.) Shoot ahead according to speed of target.

The other popular way of shooting hares is to take part in an organised drive. For this, the shooters are usually split up into 'walking guns' and 'standing guns'. The former will form a straight line and walk towards the standing guns, who will be behind some convenient cover ready to shoot the hares as they run in front of the walking guns.

If you are a walking gun you will probably be walking along with a lot of helpers—or 'beaters'—who do not carry guns but are there to assist. The closer the walkers are together, the better, because it is amazing how tight hares will sit when danger approaches, and nothing is more frustrating to all concerned than to see hares getting up behind the moving line and racing off in the opposite direction to the standing guns. It is also essential to keep the moving line straight, so that nobody can be accidentally shot when a hare gets up unexpectedly. In addition, a cardinal rule is never to follow a hare through the line with your gun. If one breaks back, keep your gun vertical until it is well clear of the line, and then bring the gun to your shoulder. Beaters do not look nice under the heading 'various' in the game book. Another thing to remember is that you should always find out before the drive begins where the standing guns are situated, so that you then take good care that you do not shoot in front of you when there is any danger of hitting the standing guns.

When it is your turn to stand and wait for the hares to come to you, choose your ground as carefully as you can. The flatter it is the better, so that you can move your feet without tripping over yourself in the process. Try to get an unrestricted view in all directions, with as few obstacles as possible to get in the way of your sight and swing.

The eyesight of the hare is not as keen as its sense of hearing, so that if you are able to stand still and blend with your surroundings the chances are that it will not see you until it is well within range. You will sometimes be able to see it running towards you from a good way off, depending upon the lie of the land, but do not make the fatal error of mounting the gun to the shoulder before you are ready to take the shot. Doing this makes one tend to aim instead of pointing and making a natural swing. Instead, wait until it is within range, and mount the gun then, and take the shot in the normal way.

If the hare is running towards you, bring the gun up behind it and swing downwards through the body, keeping your weight really well forward on the left foot, and shoot in front of it. The downward swing necessary for this shot is one which is often a little difficult to master, as it is not a natural movement, and the tendency is to jerk the gun upwards a little at the end of the swing, which will mean a miss behind. Practice will remedy this, however, especially if you can remember to keep your weight even more than usual on that left foot. The same weight technique is employed also when shooting at the hare (or anything else) when it is running from left to right, since it is harder for most shooters to bring their

left arm across the body than it is for them to swing the
other way.

When you are a standing gun always make quite sure
that you know where your companions are, and never
shoot anywhere near them, nor ever follow a hare
through the line, for the obvious reason of safety. They
should also know where you are, so do not move around
once you are in your designated position.

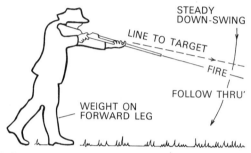

Fig. 60. (Side view of 'Coming towards' shot.) Shoot to miss in front.

Much of the foregoing can also be applied to rabbit
shooting, except that the most usual way of hunting them
is to flush them out of cover, either with a dog or with a
friend. When two of you are out together it is once more
to be stressed that one must know where the other is. So
when you are walking along one side of a hedge, keep
whistling to each other to show your positions, and never
shoot through the hedge—or through anything else which
might hide something you cannot see.

The rabbit is a smaller and more delicate target than
the hare, so it is advisable to use a smaller shot size, No.
6 for preference. It is also usually shot at closer range
than the hare, and although not so much power per pellet
is needed, a denser pattern is preferable. The usual
chance will be at a rapidly moving little bundle of fur
flashing between two sets of cover, or darting in and out

of a hedgerow. But do not let the shot be a hurried one, or you will 'poke' the gun at the target, instead of swinging through the rabbit and shooting where it is going to, rather than where it is at the time that you see it.

The other favourite ground game is—dare I mention it—the fox. One of our most daring predators, the fox is hunted by hounds and shooters alike in an effort to curtail its rampaging. Being a tough target, a larger size of shot is essential, especially as one will usually only have the chance of one shot. Number 4 shot is a good size to use, but opinions vary considerably—usually in favour of a larger shot size. If you are taking part in a fox drive through woods, and you are the standing gun on the edge of the wood do not make the error of standing out from the edge, for if 'Reynard' comes to the edge he will certainly see you and dodge back inside the wood. Stand right at the edge or just inside the wood, so that you can see without being seen, and you will have a much better chance of getting your quarry.

Remember—the rabbit is the enemy of the hare, the fox is the enemy of both and you are the enemy of all three. Jungle law prevails, in which you are the master.

WILDFOWLING

A. St. G. Tucker

The days of the professional wildfowler in this country, the halcyon days of the nineteenth and early twentieth centuries, are now just something that we read about in old books. Hawker described them—the great flocks of duck and geese surrounded by men in punts, fired upon at a given signal by great punt guns such as are seldom seen nowadays—decimated to a fraction of their numbers as the years went on.

But these days have been succeeded by a more enlightened generation of wildfowlers, men and women who have banded together into clubs and local associations, all under the Wildfowlers' Association of Great Britain and Ireland. They protect shooting around our coasts, practise conservation and breeding and see to it that the laws regarding protected birds are adhered to, surely a much healthier attitude than the indiscriminate and thoughtless slaughter of our forefathers.

The Wildfowlers' Association (popularly called 'WAGBI') has done an enormous amount to educate this section of the shooting public in recent years, and is constantly fighting battles and generally looking after its members. As such it is well worth supporting by the small annual subscription, which should be sent to the Secretary of the Association.

There are several facets of wildfowling in Great Britain and, depending on your circumstances and where you live, you may enjoy the morning flight or the evening flight on saltwater or freshwater marshes, an inland flight pond or merely on the coast. Each has its own appeal, and it is remarkable where one can enjoy wildfowling for no more expense than a few hours spent in search and enquiry.

Until quite recently there has been a tendency to suppose that the ordinary game gun is of little use on a wildfowling trip. Subsequently fowlers have gone out with guns which were so heavy they could hardly be lifted, and shot that was very large. The number of pellets in each cartridge was thus so small that the pattern at forty yards was sufficiently spread out to permit a whole skein of geese to fly through it unscathed. All this has led to the belief that birds way up in the sky were quite within range of these well-stoked gaspipes, and the subsequent generation of 'marsh-cowboys', who work on the principle that 'if it is in sight, it is in range', has spoiled the sport in a good many areas, most notably the Wash.

The logic behind the argument of the 'big gunners' is that the larger the cartridge, the more shot there is in the air, and therefore it must be more effective. And naturally the larger the cartridge, the larger must be the gun. All this is indeed logical, but a closer examination is necessary. Naturally the larger the shot size, the fewer pellets there are in comparison with the same type of cartridge holding a smaller size of shot. It is equally true to say that the larger the shot size, the more striking energy there is in each individual pellet, and it will also lose this energy less quickly than a smaller pellet. Therefore, when using the larger sizes of shot, necessary to kill a goose for instance, it is necessary to have a larger cartridge so that more pellets can be fired per charge of shot in order that the pattern is not spread out too much at long ranges.

It is therefore far more satisfactory to use a gun which is not too heavy for you and cartridges in that gun loaded with a shot size that will: (a) be large enough to kill the bird, and (b) throw a good pattern at long range. Although shot sizes 1 and 3 are recommended for geese, they can just as well be shot with a much smaller size given the right conditions, so do not sacrifice everything for extreme range, for it is simply not worth it. You may hit the bird at very long ranges, but the chances are that it will fly on with the shot in its body and later die in agony.

Wildfowling has a magic all of its own, and those who pursue it form a little branch of select shooters. Going out in all weathers often to places that ordinary folk would shun even at the best of times, they get really close to nature, and count the hardships they endure as part of the fun of the sport.

When going out for the first time it is most inadvisable to go on your own, for the dangers of the sport do not warrant it. Go with someone who knows the area, and

can act as your guide for a while. He will—or should— know the state of the tides (let us here deal with coastal shooting, for that is the commonest form of fowling), the best locations to go to and can pass on to you many more useful tips that have been learned by experience.

The clothes which you wear will depend on the weather, but the overall effect must be one by which you will merely become part of the terrain. It is advisable to wear a hat, since it will hide your face from anything flying over, and a camouflaged face mask is a necessity for daytime shooting or under the moon. It is amazing how a face will shine out of your otherwise perfect camouflage unless it is covered. Your jacket should be a neutral green or brown, and preferably water and wind-proof. Wear an old pair of trousers, again of a neutral colour, but not necessarily waterproof. For marsh fowl-ing, waders are essential, and excellent things to wear with these are waterproof knee-length shorts, so that you can then sit down without getting a wet seat and yet walk without impediment. Mittens or special shooting gloves are necessary too not only for warmth but also to camouflage the hands, but the trigger finger and the thumb which operates the safety catch or hammers must not be impeded. What you wear under these outer gar-ments is a matter of personal preference, but the general rule is warmth and comfort without restriction of move-ments. Wearing too many socks, for example, will merely mean that your feet are firmly wedged in your waders and cannot move at all to help circulation, and too many clothes above the belt will hinder movement when firing.

Other useful odds and ends that can easily be stowed in one's game bag include a collapsible cleaning rod or pull-through in case your barrels get mud or some other blockage in them; a hand-warmer if the weather is very cold; an oily rag to wipe the gun down; a length of rope or cord; a knife; a flask of spirits to warm the inner man; a compass and a torch. Too many wildfowlers think it 'cissy' to cater for personal comfort, but I for one enjoy my shooting more if I am comfortable.

I have already mentioned something about guns, but a few more words on the subject will not come amiss. Sea air and salt water do not improve a gun at all, since both are very corrosive, so that it is obvious that wildfowling does not call for an expensive weapon. My ideal wild-fowling gun is a boxlock non-ejector with full choke in the left barrel and half choke in the right. Chamber length and barrel length are merely a question of choice. I do not favour an automatic weapon for the 'messy' type of fowling, having seen several rendered useless on the marsh when they and their owners are sprawled in the mud. Besides which I always like to be able to slip in a larger size of shot if geese are heard to be approaching, which is difficult with an automatic. The fact is that the less there is to go wrong with a wildfowling gun, the better. When you get off the marsh at the end of the 'flight' (the most recognised times for wildfowling are when the fowl are flying out to sea or in from the sea, i.e. at dusk and dawn) give the gun a wipe over with an oily rag, and when you get indoors your very first task should be to go over the weapon really thoroughly to remove all traces of mud and salt water, besides scrubbing out the inside of the barrels. A regular visit to the gun-maker to have the action stripped and cleaned, the barrels reblacked, and any traces of pitting removed at the outset can put years of life to your gun, so that the small expenditure involved is well worthwhile.

Of further assistance to the wildfowler are the various bird calls and decoys which are on the market. One can purchase calls for mallard, wigeon, teal and geese which can be of very great assistance if used correctly. Duck decoys are also used very extensively to attract their live counterparts who do not realise until too late, if at all, that 'they are not what they are painted'. Only a few decoys are required, except on a large expanse of water, and they are very reasonably priced. Nearly all types available in this country are made of rubber, and can be anchored by the attachment of a weighted cord, so that they will face into the wind (as a live duck will) and ride the waves in a really lifelike manner. One will usually use these decoys where the duck are known to feed, so choose your pool by looking for the droppings and flattened grass round the edges. Then hide yourself preferably in a handy creek or gully so that you can see the ducks as they come in to land on the pool, remembering that they will land into the wind. Thus you should wait for them

with the wind blowing into your face, wherever the pond is in relation to your hide. Needless to say, one should never wait until the duck has landed before firing . . .!

When going on to the marsh, when leaving the marsh and when you are on the marsh always remember that there are probably other wildfowlers about, and any unnecessary noise, flashing of torches or walking about can ruin their sport and enjoyment. There are usually one or two people around who ruin the flight for everyone else, but make sure that you are not one of them.

Now that the country as a whole has become more

'conservation minded' and the Protection of Birds Act, 1954, has become law it is essential that you should know what birds you may shoot and what birds you may not shoot. Your local Wildfowlers Club will be able to help you, or you can write direct to the British Field Sports Society at 51 Victoria Street, London, S.W.1.

THE PIGEON

Maurice Turner

The wood-pigeon, the 'poor man's pheasant', is one of the enigmas of nature. It is such a common sight in the British Isles that it will need no description here.

It is persecuted throughout the year, yet regularly invades these shores in its hundreds and thousands to molest the farmers' crops, irritate small-holders and play havoc with peas and other vegetables in private gardens.

The female lays only two white eggs at a sitting, but she disregards seasons and hatches out her young indiscriminately when other birds have given up all thoughts of rearing families. This may account for the wood-pigeon's continued existence despite the massive numbers which are slaughtered.

Vast hordes migrate from the Continent in the autumn, and these birds are a smaller variety than the British resident. When nesting the plump, light grey male of our own species is easily identified, and can be recognised when wooing his mate by his flying display of a steep upward climb with wings audibly flapping, a stall, then a graceful downward glide towards his wife-to-be. At this time the pigeon becomes more confiding and 'coos' lovingly in nearby trees. Otherwise it is wary and very much on the alert.

The wood-pigeon is a godsend to the novice sportsman who is not afraid to expend a certain amount on cartridges. It provides free sport, a wide variety of shots and is as tough a bird to bring down as any in these Islands. It is classified as vermin, so can be shot throughout the year, and being a cunning rascal, can be outwitted by the beginner only if he studies its habits, learns something about woodcraft and is possessed of infinite patience. He must also brave the elements, as the best pigeon shooting is obtained on wintry windy days. Then he must camouflage himself with appropriate clothing, even to blacking his face with a burnt cork or, if this idea does not appeal, making himself a face mask from some old bit of dull green material. The hands, too, should not be overlooked and be streaked with burnt cork or, if preferred, green mittens can be worn. Alternatively, the beginner can fit himself out with all necessary accoutrements for pigeon shooting at that excellent shop in Piccadilly, Cogswell & Harrison.

Nowadays organised pigeon-shoots are frequently arranged on, virtually, a county basis. Numerous guns turn out on a given day and, under the direction of area organisers, as much cover as possible is manned, with the intention of harrying the pigeon from pillar to post so that it gains no respite and receives inhospitable treatment wherever it goes. Frankly, I would not advise the novice sportsman to join in these big organised days to start with. He may see only distant pigeon, and what shots he does get may be so infrequent that he learns little or nothing, and ends his day by classifying pigeon-shooting as an over-rated pastime. But nearly all farmers warmly welcome and encourage sportsmen to wage war on the pigeon, particularly when crops are ripening or tender shoots are showing. If our novice has already acquired his rough shoot, then he owes it as a duty to his landlord to turn out regularly with his little syndicate to keep the 'cushat' host in check.

Let us hope, anyway, that our beginner is keen enough to want to put in some out-of-season shooting practice and, with a friend or two to cover strategic points, pit his wits against a keen-sighted, sharp-witted quarry.

It is as well, if not essential, to ascertain at first on what crops the flocks, against which war is to be declared, are battening. When these are known the pigeons' feeding habits and the times of day when they are on the move must be studied. Their line of flight must be noted, and here again wind plays its part, as pigeon usually approach their feeding grounds up-wind after, most probably, a circuit or two of the surrounding area.

When the movements of the birds and their feeding habits have been watched by the beginner he can then decide how he is going to tackle the problem of shooting them. If he has roped in enough friends he may decide to restrict his guns to the coverts. If, on the other hand, he is confident about his timing and the line of flight he may choose to select a place for a hide and try his luck on birds flying from coverts to the feeding grounds, and vice versa. Again he may prefer the hour of dusk to shoot roosting pigeon with, often, the best results if there is blustery weather and flocks are coming in low. Despite bitter cold and high winds, I have had some memorable evenings with a few friends when pigeon have streamed in to roost till it was too dark to see and, regardless of

salvos to right and left, finally forced their way into the coverts to pitch all anyhow in the trees beyond the guns.

Big flocks often, if not always, will send spies ahead to look around and give the 'all clear'. These fore-runners should be left unmolested and the guns freeze still as death when they are circling round.

Last, but by no means least, the use of decoys is favoured by very many sportsmen, and produces good results. Modern decoys are excellent imitations, and balanced so that the wind sets them rocking in a most life-like pecking motion. They should be set out down-wind from the sportsman's hide, which will be less conspicuous if he positions himself up-wind of his chosen landing area. Pigeon, after reconnaissance, will finally turn in to land up-wind, and the decoys should, consequently, face more or less into the wind, not in 'column o' lumps' but dispersed and angled naturally. About six decoys should be ample for the novice sportsman to make a 'show'.

Again I would recommend, if possible, a visit to Cogswell & Harrison, who sell a variety of decoys at reasonable prices. They can also provide portable hides which save a great deal of preparation.

When a pigeon or two have been bagged it does no harm to put them out among the decoys. Sticks and twigs can be used to support them and give them a natural appearance, and a dead one may advantageously be set out with wings and tail spread to simulate a landing bird. As in all pigeon shooting, a blustery day is better than a dead calm one for shooting over decoys.

But whatever method the novice sportsman may adopt to get within range of this worthy, though common, adversary, let it never be under-rated as a sporting bird. The pigeon's senses seem to be uncannily over-developed, and it is always suspicious of anything strange within its sight, which is exceptionally keen. An ill-timed movement, a flash from the sun on a pair of glasses or an ill-considered noise may send a flock suddenly skywards and ruin an hour or more of patient approach or waiting.

As a target, it may test the novice's skill at any time or season by flying over him high and fast, or by planing in to roost comparatively slowly, only to climb and twist away at full throttle as the gun is raised to the shoulder.

If, though, the sportsman is really well camouflaged and hidden and the flighting pigeon is flying unhurried and nicely within range it does not present too difficult a mark. But it carries a surprising amount of shot and, unless killed stone dead, will often turn completely over in the air, recover and fly on as though unharmed. If a large number of cartridges are fired at flighting or roosting pigeon inevitably quite a high percentage of wounded birds will fly on out of sight to drop stone dead up to five or six hundred yards beyond the gun's hide to be picked up, possibly, by somebody else the next day.

What, to me, is one of the hardest shots in the world is at the pigeon which suddenly jumps out of a tree after methodically working its way round to the opposite side as the sportsman approaches. It allows only a snap-shot, yet the temptation to fire is always irresistible! The pigeon will offer just such a shot often enough, but if a hit is registered more than once in ten times the sportsman can congratulate himself!

Lightning shooting is also essential when walking up pigeon within a wood. This is good entertainment, as pigeon seem to have a knack of putting every possible obstacle between themselves and the gun. The sportsman gets only glimpses of his target between the boughs overhead, and has to place his shot into an open space with split-second precision. I always damage a lot more tree-trunks than pigeon when indulging in this pastime, and would advise the beginner to save his cartridges until he has mastered the more simple shots!

I would advocate No. 6 shot for the pigeon, although his downy covering is such that some sportsmen prefer the more penetrating qualities of No. 4. It is a matter of personal preference, but none of us likes to leave behind more wounded birds than necessary, even vermin. Fours do more bodily damage to pigeon than sixes, while the percentage of 'pick-ups' is not likely to be greatly different whichever shot is used, so I would advise the novice to keep to the same size of shot for pigeon as he uses for game-birds.

Very often a well-fed dead pigeon will burst its crop when it hits the ground with a thud, and it will probably surprise the novice sportsman to discover just how much an over-indulged bird will swallow and store! Little wonder that the farmer gets alarmed when his land is invaded by thousands of birds with voracious appetites and pleads for war on the pigeon to be waged unabated throughout the year.

It might be appropriate now to mention vermin other than pigeon, as the novice sportsman must keep a wary eye open for predators which can play havoc with game-birds, particularly in the breeding season.

All hawks and falcons, as well as owls, are now on the protected list, and sad it is that the once all too common kestrel and sparrow-hawk have almost disappeared from our countryside, as their blood-streams have gradually absorbed the poisons in the modern manures and pesticides through the medium of their natural prey.

But many predatory birds and animals have avoided contact with these pollutions and continue to thrive. Those harmful to game can legitimately be destroyed, and the zealous novice will see to it that his syndicate pull their weight in turning out after the close of the season to take part in vermin shoots.

The hen pheasant and partridge are helpless and vulnerable birds when sitting on eggs or looking after young chicks. They will easily be driven or lured from the nest by any of half a dozen or so enemies which will destroy a clutch of eggs or play havoc with a young brood in a matter of seconds.

Of these by far the most harmful is the fox. Deprived of its staple diet, the rabbit, the fox looks to any form of sustenance to keep it alive and, if well established in a covert, will destroy countless pheasants in and out of season. In days gone by it was almost a crime to shoot a

fox, which was considered to be a prerequisite of the local hunt. Today the fox is shot out of hand, and every effort should be made to discourage the intrusion of this very harmful animal into pheasant-holding woods.

The grey squirrel, stoat and weasel, if allowed to multiply, will poach the syndicate's reserves, and should be shot on sight. There should be no compunction about loosing off a couple of barrels at a grey-squirrel's 'dray' if one is discovered in the breeding season.

Badgers, if found, should, I think, be spared. There is some controversy about the amount of harm that badgers do to livestock, but give them the benefit of the doubt, I say, if a pair do make their appearance.

Of the birds, the carrion-crow is a fearful robber and cruel miscreant, and if its nest is located it should be given the two-barrel treatment. Pretty as they may appear, the jay and magpie are evil thieves, and no good shoot supports any more than the odd one or two which have escaped attention.

It is probably just as well to be too harsh with vermin rather than over-lenient, but I do not support the game-keeper who deals in indiscriminate slaughter and kills practically everything that crosses his foresight. It is, for instance, quite unnecessary to shoot gulls and cuckoos, both of which I have seen in game-keepers' larders.

So when the novice has acquired his ground he has taken on an absorbing interest for twelve months of the year, and his gun need seldom be put away for long.

But if he meets frustration at the start of his shooting career, yet is an enthusiast and has selected his weapon, then I can only emphasise that he can obtain all the pigeon shooting he wants without looking far afield. He will fire off plenty of cartridges and get the 'feel' of his gun and, if he is observant, learn some valuable field and woodcraft, which will stand him in good stead when the partridge and pheasant shooting do eventually come his way.

Let him remember, also, that the wood-pigeon makes a very welcome and appetising change of diet when game is out of season.

THE GROUSE

Maurice Turner

There are four distinct species of grouse in the British Isles, the Red Grouse, Ptarmigan, Black Grouse and Capercaillie.

Of these, the first two, like the partridge, are monogamous and pair off early in spring to rear and form a family covey. The Black Grouse and Capercaillie, on the other hand, make much ado of quarrelling for their several wives at the beginning of the mating season, and woo their hens with a lot of showy display and courtship.

The Red Grouse, confined to Britain, is by far the most abundant of the four, and is also the most widely dispersed, being found on most moors and hills in Scotland, in Northern England, particularly in Yorkshire, but as far south as Shropshire and in various counties of Wales. There, also, dwells the Black Grouse, where suitable conditions exist.

To start with, we shall confine ourselves to the Red Grouse, with which the beginner will first familiarise himself if he wants to assemble his gun and fill his cartridge bag with his No. 6 in preparation for 'the glorious twelfth'.

The Red Grouse is dependent on a good growth of young heather and the cranberry plant for its living, but it looks to other wild berries, grass seeds, corn in season and tender green shoots for its existence, and also likes water and plenty of grit to be at hand.

It has made a remarkable recovery since the war, during which vermin and neglect virtually wiped it out in several parts of the country. Being a dweller of the open, the Red Grouse is most vulnerable to the attacks of its natural enemies, particularly the fox, which can play havoc on a moor which is not keepered or otherwise controlled.

The female nests in late April or early May in some well-sheltered hollow lined with grass and moss. She lays up to a dozen eggs, and her chicks look to insects to form their staple diet in their early life.

This grouse may not be as familiar to the novice sportsman as is the partridge and pheasant, so I will attempt to describe it briefly. It varies according to locality, but, generally, the cock is a rich dark red, broken with lines and small patches of black which include some buff on the upper parts of the body. The breast is whitish or flecked with white, and there is a white patch on the head at the joint of the beak. The legs are white and fluffy and are transformed into brooches for female adornment!

This magnificent game-bird has a scarlet comb which is enlarged during the breeding season, when the cock likes to show off his rich spring plumage and spread his tail fan-wise to attract his chosen lady-friend.

The female is a lighter red or, often, a yellowish brown, with more noticeable black markings and buff and white in her plumage.

Both sexes moult at, oddly enough, different months of the year, but during the shooting season the cock is not so showily dressed as in the breeding season.

The Red Grouse is a larger and heavier bird than the partridge, and the beginner could not possibly fail to identify his first covey, even if the old cock bird did not give tongue and order the line of guns to 'Go-back, go-back, go-back, go-back, go-back'!

Unless the novice sportsman lives near suitable moorland country, he will have to be content with shooting his grouse during his annual holidays. It is not, like the pheasant and partridge, a Saturday game-bird, as few of us these days can afford to travel far by night and incur heavy expense on numerous week-ends during a year, as well as pull our weight in a near-at-home syndicate.

So if the novice is determined to take out his gun on the twelfth of August he must arrange his holiday accordingly and make his plans well in advance. He will not, obviously, consider the complications and high cost of renting a moor for a restricted period, even if one became available. So he must study the advertisements in the sporting papers for hotels or such organisations in Scotland, Northern England or Wales which hold the shooting rights over some moorland, and make daily or weekly charges to visiting guns either on a flat basis for a day's or week's sport or on the size of the bag obtained.

But the novice will find that the best of these organisations are booked well ahead by 'regulars', if there is worthwhile shooting to be had, so he must make his preparations, if possible, eight or ten months in advance. If he delays until, say, May or June to book in at a hotel with some alleged shooting available, and is offered a room, he can be almost certain that he will find he is trudging through old heather until his calves are knotted, perhaps to put up one small covey of grouse during a whole day! There will probably be nobody to guide his footsteps, and certainly no trained dogs.

If, though, the beginner has given himself time in hand he will be able to study past records of bags which the honest hotel manager is only too willing to advertise if his moors are a feature of his hospitality.

I remember only too vividly my first introduction to grouse shooting, which I obtained, through the help of a good friend, on some hotel moors in Wales. Shoots, with a keeper, were arranged on alternate days, trained setters were available and three pounds per day was charged for each gun, usually six in number, for a day's walking up over dogs. These days normally ended with a bag of twelve brace or so.

There were neighbouring moors which were driven, and hotel gun-guests could, by arrangement, take part in a day's driving, which usually resulted in fifty or sixty brace. The charge was only five pounds per gun.

Such bags are very modest in relation to the big Scottish and Yorkshire moors, but that was a memorable holiday, on which I killed my first grouse and tore my first black-cock out of the sky with a long shot which I shall never forget!

On non-shooting days you were invited to try out the hotel trout fishing, or exercise yourself with a gun over rough ground and shoot rabbit and pigeon and, perhaps, the straying grouse as well.

I have returned to this haunt of my boyhood days on more than one occasion. The grouse disappeared from those moors almost entirely during the war, but on my last visit bags of ten and twelve brace were again being obtained over dogs, and a keeper had gained control over the vermin which had bred, unchecked, for several years.

The charge for walking-up birds had been increased to five pounds per gun for a day exceeding ten brace. It was proportionately less for smaller bags.

I would therefore recommend to the novice sportsman that he should endeavour to discover a hotel such as this, introduce himself to the grouse by walking it up over dogs with, if not a keeper, somebody who knows the territory and to leave the driven bird alone for his first season or two unless, of course, small impromptu drives can be organised to vary the shooting during the day.

It is fascinating to watch pointers or setters at work on a moor. When the leading dog 'freezes', with front paw raised, 'backed up' by the dog behind, having scented a covey, there are tense moments as the adjacent guns inch forward behind the forward dog and the flank guns wheel inwards. The covey suddenly explodes out of the heather in range of, maybe, three guns, and a halt is called while the dead birds are retrieved, which is a welcome respite to one or two of us unconditioned as yet to trudging heather and hillsides.

Wind and weather probably play their part in grouse shooting more than in the pursuit of any other game-bird. But your novice, or even experienced sportsman, will be most unlikely to find himself in sole charge of a grouse shoot, mainly because the time factor does not give him a chance to get to know the terrain unless he actually owns it. He must therefore rely on a keeper or knowledgeable local man to advise him. There are obviously basic rules to be observed.

In olden times rarely more than two guns walked up grouse over dogs, but nowadays the keeper or shoot's manager may be handling a line of six or eight guns. Thus a lot more territory is covered more haphazardly and less thoroughly than in olden times. When shooting over dogs the line would obviously not approach birds down-wind, as a dog can only pick up a scent from birds lying up or across wind of him. Weather can vary tremendously in grouse country, and birds will not lie, for example, on the most exposed hillsides if half a gale is blowing.

Grouse coveys tend to fly downhill when put up, so the line should work the higher ground first and not scatter the coveys and lose birds by 'taking it easy' on the lower slopes because a climb first thing after breakfast is a bit of a strain on wind and limb!

Dogs, when they point, will normally indicate the direction from which they have picked up the scent. But if there is a slanting or cross wind the dog may appear to be questing with his nose to discover from exactly where the scent is reaching him. This may often mean that the covey is lying uphill of the dogs, and the guns on the high extremity of the line should wheel slowly downhill, while the lower flank guns edge forward prepared for shots at some fast-moving birds!

Walking-up without dogs is not quite so enthralling, except that the grouse, at home on his moor, is essentially a bird of the wild, and there is far more exercise involved in coming to terms with him than with the partridge. The rules which govern the shooting of the grouse on foot are bound to be more elastic owing to the very nature of the ground on which this bird lives. Fields can be walked up according to wind and weather, but the steep heathery hillside will present its problems on windy inclement days, and the novice can be guided only by the man on the spot. The dour Scottish keeper can, though, be as stubborn as his 'Sassenach' brother, and will cover territory one way, and one way only, just because he has always stuck to a hidebound programme!

But if it be remembered that wind, as always, plays its part whether walking-up or driving, that grouse tend to fly downhill rather than up and will get away from draughty places if there is shelter round the corner, then the novice can at least voice his opinion if he thinks he is paying for obstinate mismanagement of a precious day's shooting. The Red Grouse is not a difficult target when he rises at close range, but, like the partridge, will soon be on the watch for intruders after a disturbance or two.

I cannot usefully endeavour to add anything to what has been written elsewhere in this book which will help the beginner to kill his first few grouse, assuming that he has already had some experience with a rough shoot.

Partridge and grouse both rise from the ground in coveys and, although some sportsmen consider that the latter take to the wing more slowly, the newcomer to the moor will barely notice the difference, and should not attempt to vary such tactics as he may have already practised.

There is one large 'but'! Whereas the partridge dwells

in gentlemanly fashion on nice flat fields, the grouse frequents heathery hillsides. The novice sportsman, trudging through moorland along the side of a steep hill, will not often have time, when a covey rises, to correct his stance to take his weight on his left foot. He may be caught with one foot in the air and his weight thrown backwards, and must be prepared to fire from such awkward positions in which heather and hillside have combined to place him. A moderately bare hillside which may hold grouse in its patches of cover can be extremely slippery, and at times it is all that the sportsman can do to keep upright. But a little experience will tell, and the beginner will soon master the art of firing from all kinds of stances, even though he only just avoids sitting down hard a dozen times during the day!

Driving grouse presents a different problem altogether, and the novice is even more dependent on guidance from others. Drivers, too, must be perfectly controlled. For one thing, the moor is not subdivided into fields like farm land, so a limited number of coveys cannot so easily be isolated and driven, like partridges, over guns taking a stance behind hedges.

Butts, six or possibly eight in number, which are, so to speak, small gun emplacements made usually from lumps of peat, are built in line abreast of the drive. To these the guns repair and stand camouflaged, and do not see the beaters, who are bringing in outlying moor to assemble grouse coveys in the operational area, over a distance of, possibly, three miles. While the guns are taking up their positions they may disturb grouse in the immediate vicinity. This does not matter, because such coveys will, in all probability, settle again in the area to be driven that day and, later, come high and fast and well dispersed over the butts.

According to the moor, and the weather, flanking drivers may be needed, and these may be just in sight of the guns and, for some time, provide the only evidence that there is activity beyond the slope ahead. The beaters' flags, to help turn birds which are trying to break back are, eventually, seen in the distance, and from then onwards shooting may become fast and furious!

It stands to reason, though, that there are usually more complications in grouse driving than in the organisation of partridge shoots. Consequently, there are far fewer grouse drives organised for a single day—three or four only—although the total area actually driven may be greater than is covered during a day of partridge driving.

There is such a variety of moorland throughout England, Scotland and Wales that it is not possible to write in a short chapter what rules apply to the art of driving the grouse. The very nature of the hills themselves govern the method to be employed, and I can only, once again, refer the reader to the several old books, devoted by the old masters to the grouse, in which the killing of up to a thousand brace in a day is mentioned and described.

Space allows me only a few brief words on the other species.

The Ptarmigan, which changes its plumage from brownish grey, black and white in the breeding season, to pure white in the winter, is found in these isles in Scotland only, where it inhabits the somewhat inhospitable top and stony slopes of the mountains. Its range extends into Europe as far south as the Pyrenees, and species occur in North America and Northern Asia.

The Ptarmigan is not harried as rigorously as the Red Grouse owing to the exacting uphill scramble required to reach its territory. Early in the season it affords an easy mark, as it is inclined to rely on its camouflage to hide it and squats until put up at close range. It is just the reverse in its white dress, when it becomes extremely wild and wary.

The novice sportsman may well relish the climb required to reach the Ptarmigan's hilltops, and good luck to him if he enjoys a day or two in its pursuit.

The Blackcock is a magnificent bird on the decrease, alas, in many parts of Scotland, Northern England and Wales. This splendid creature is well known for his lyre-shaped tail, and the habit known as 'lekking', which is the assembly of the cocks in the spring to display their plumage and do battle for their wives.

Its range extends throughout most of Europe and Scandinavia.

Black-game haunt the countryside where there is birch-wood and an abundance of heather adjacent to pasture and open land known, romantically, as 'the fringe of the moor'. In his pursuit of the Red Grouse, the novice sportsman may well be led into country which holds

these birds, and one or two Blackcock in the bag among
the other grouse are always a pleasing addition.

The female, the Greyhen, is usually spared by the
sportsman throughout the season, which opens for black-
game on the twentieth of August.

These birds are unmistakable for their slow wing-flap
in flight, although their speed is very deceptive. They are,
also, larger than the Red Grouse.

Finally comes the largest of all grouse, the famous
'Caper'. Also on the decrease, this fine bird loves forest-
land, principally Scots pine, but it lives too among larch
and birch.

The cock 'Caper' is another dandy that carries on his
courtship in a tree, where he spreads his tail, flaps his
wings and makes ugly harsh calls which could only
sound pleasing to a hen Capercaillie!

This bird has had a hazardous career, and was virtually extinct in these Islands till reintroduced not much
more than a hundred years ago. In Scotland the novice
sportsman is unlikely to obtain an early chance of joining

in 'Caper' shoots. Nowadays only the favoured few are invited to attend them or else pay handsomely for the privilege of taking part in such shooting as includes these birds.

The Capercaillie is found also in Scandinavia and Russia and in various European localities southwards to Italy and Spain.

THE PARTRIDGE

Maurice Turner

Just a word or two about the Grey Partridge.

Widely distributed throughout the country, it favours light sandy soil such as is found in Norfolk and surrounding counties, where the largest bags are nowadays obtained. It breeds freely throughout the Continent and in parts of Asia Minor, and appears in various guises in many parts of the Tropics.

In the British Isles this partridge pairs usually in February, when the cock is at his most vociferous generally at dawn and dusk. If times become hard after birds have paired they will frequently re-form coveys until conditions improve.

The hen lays up to twenty eggs from late April onwards, and the chicks leave the nest as soon as they are hatched. They stay with their parents, and thus the covey is formed, although later in the year small coveys may amalgamate.

The grey partridge is too well known to need a full description from me. The sexes vary slightly, in that the female is browner than the male, and the cock can be identified by the large brown 'horse-shoe' on his breast. This is missing altogether from the hen or is much smaller.

I must introduce the Red-legged or French Partridge, which is believed to have been nationalised towards the end of the eighteenth century. It mainly frequents the Southern and Eastern Counties, and although it has the reputation of being quarrelsome, seems to live in harmony with its grey brother. Its range is not nearly so wide as the other and is confined principally to Europe.

The 'Frenchman' is inclined to run when driven, but is strong on the wing, although it favours short flights. Its nesting habits are similar to the Grey Partridge, except that the hen lays somewhat fewer eggs.

This bird is easily identified by its heavily and colourfully barred flanks and red beak and legs. Both sexes are almost similar.

But to revert to the Grey Partridge.

It was not long ago when the 'little brown bird' was as much a heritage of our countryside as the meadows which it frequented."

But now it is steadily fighting a losing battle. Land is valuable, costs are rising and the farmer has to exploit every productive foot of his property. In the process he is gradually destroying the hedgerows and patches of cover which once gave sanctuary to the nesting partridge.

Add to this the wholesale destruction of weeds and insects by modern fertilisers and insecticides, and a lot of the partridge's natural food is eliminated from the soil. Where small-holdings produced, perhaps, three or four coveys from carefully preserved headlands it is rare, nowadays, in many districts to startle a single covey into flight during a long country ramble.

But there are still many farmers, landlords, some Co-operative Societies and National Reserves controlling various acreages who sell the shooting rights of their properties based, usually, on so much per acre. This can vary from some fifty pence to several pounds, dependent, largely, on what shooting prospects are offered, but there is no hard-and-fast rule.

His search for somewhere to make a start to his shooting career will call for hard work and bring disappointment to the novice sportsman, as competition these days is keen. He would be well advised to advertise in sporting and local papers, not only for rough shooting but also for vacancies in small syndicates, keep eyes and ears open, and scour the adjacent countryside in his spare time in late winter or early spring to discover those precious few hundred acres of arable and woodland which are fundamental.

We will pretend that luck holds for our beginner in this chapter, and that he finds one or two promising openings. He should not pay too much attention to the landlords' optimism about their stock of game, and take nothing for granted. A walk round his selected areas when there is

yet no greenery and cover is bare will soon disclose the
stock those areas are likely to hold later in the year, and
he can assess their value accordingly. If there is evidence
by the presence of a few pairs of partridge or a covey or
two not yet dispersed, then he can look forward to taking
his gun, presumably already selected, from its case early
in September. When it is time to lay in his supply of
ammunition he will require No. 6 shot, so need purchase
nothing for partridge shooting that will not last him
throughout the season.

By September the first, then, the beginner will have
formed his own little syndicate and be ready on that day
of days to place his guns with a few stalwart friends to
act as beaters. Early in the season, and on a rough shoot
of limited acreage holding just a few coveys partridges
are usually what is known as 'walked-up', as opposed to
being driven over the guns in prepared positions. That is
guns and beaters walk the fields in line, putting up the
birds ahead of them, with the sportsmen so spaced that
nothing can get up out of range between the guns.

There are several fields of stubble, grass, plough and
roots to be walked over on our shoot and, with a limited
number of birds to provide the day's sport, care must be
taken to keep them within its boundaries. Before
September is old and the coveys have not been unduly
disturbed, partridges can usually be 'disciplined' fairly
easily. But if put up carelessly they may naturally fly on
to somebody else's land if it suits them and be lost for the
rest of the day. Early in the season a covey will not often
travel any great distance, and can usually be coerced to
fly in the required direction by making use of forward
flank guns. In other words, two guns go forward of the
line on each flank, and the birds, rather than run the
gauntlet of the flankers, will fly forward where they are
intended to go. Walking up across wind should, if possible, be avoided, as like most winged game, partridges
have a preference for flying directly up- or down-wind.

If a few coveys can thus be found during a day and exploited strategically they can give endless entertainment to a small party of guns. Patience must be exercised though, and a covey, marked down again after it has been once fired upon, will rise far out of range if it is immediately pursued. The birds must be given time to recover from a startling disturbance and put up again after the guns have covered other ground which has, no doubt, in its turn, provided its own diversions.

Let me here digress for just so long as it takes me to impress on the beginner the necessity of controlling his line of guns and beaters. This should be kept strictly under surveillance, and the line halted and reformed if it gets out of hand. A careless or 'dreamy' gun who perpetually gets ahead of or behind the line is an annoyance to the rest of the shoot and not only ruins the shooting but also subscribes towards accidents. Another chapter in this book has been devoted to gun safety, nevertheless a slap-happy individual in the line is a menace and a danger. If the beginner is controlling his shoot, then he must keep his line constantly in check and watch his flank guns as well, as they can easily wander too far ahead. When game gets up and is killed, then, obviously, the whole line halts until the dead are collected and then re-forms.

Your more blasé sportsman may say that the walked-up partridge provides poor shooting and a limited variety of shots. Early in the season, when coveys are inclined to sit until the line is well within range, it may be true that the partridge is a reasonably easy target. But as the days pass, and the coveys have been disturbed a few times and, perhaps, lost a few of their members, they become a very different proposition, rising steeply just within range or, as frequently happens, breaking up and taking to the wing singly or in pairs. Often a covey can then be seen 'legging it' ahead of the line and then scattering in the air in all directions. There may even be some 'kamakazis' who will try their luck at breaking back! The birds can afterwards be heard calling to each other until the covey is re-formed.

Time wears on, and the birds become wilder. The novice member of a rough shoot begins to appreciate that, with finance strained and stock too limited to be driven by paid beaters, he must look upon those early September days as interludes to fill in gaps before the season proper starts. But it is still worth turning out in the early autumn to trudge the fields for a shot or two at ground game and pigeon, and improvise drives with the limited resources of man-power available whenever coveys are marked down.

Again your more blasé sportsman may tell you that it is not worth the time and energy involved in outwitting just a covey or two with barely a fifty–fifty chance of success. But we are not yet concerned with large bags and sore shoulders, but turn out for the fun which our modest little shoot can provide.

Maybe less than a half a dozen coveys are marked down on days such as these, and the strength of some of them may be but a few birds. Nevertheless, it gives great satisfaction to outwit a wily covey with the strategic use of flankers and the careful placing of guns, even though wide time-consuming detours may have to be worked out to avoid a disturbance before the signal can be given for the beaters to advance. But we pack up when the sun is sinking, healthily tired and happy, and drive contentedly home with a brace of birds, a hare and a pigeon or two in the boot of the car as an offering to a neglected wife! Perhaps the sitting-room should have been given that long overdue coat of paint, but now it will probably have to wait until February!

So if the beginner has been fortunate enough to rent or otherwise acquire just a few hundred acres of rough shooting which will yield a mixed bag he should, for a beginner, rest content.

A dog is a tremendous asset where there is scrub, woodland and overgrown ditches. Wounded partridges, particularly 'Frenchmen' and, alas, there must always be a few, will invariably make for cover, and when once a wounded bird has gone to ground it is virtually irrecoverable without a dog.

But a dog can play havoc with a day's shooting if it is turned loose, untrained, to range the countryside at will. I have been present on a number of occasions when a guest gun has turned up with a spaniel or retriever. Tactful enquiries have elicited the response that the dog has a magnificent pedigree and its great grandfather was a field-trial champion, ergo, it must be a wonderful gun-dog!

Such a dog usually behaves itself till the first hare bobs up. Then it is off, and guns resignedly lower their weapons. Its owner smites his brow and declares that this is the very first time such a thing has happened. The dog returns in time, having wrecked the next three-quarters of an hour's shooting, and is cautioned until its owner's throat is sore. A sign of complete lack of training reveals itself when the dog rolls on its back and sticks its paws in the air. It spends the rest of the day leashed to its master's belt, lugging him, protesting audibly, across the fields, and by lunch-time everybody has become irritable. But a well-trained dog, or at least one that does not run in, does not shy at thick cover and can retrieve is worth, at times, several untrained beaters.

I need say little about keepered shoots and expensive syndicates. The novice sportsman can very rarely winkle himself into a long-established partridge shoot and is, because of his inexperience, unlikely to be invited as a guest by any of the landed gentry. So his chances of firing innumerable cartridges at big partridge drives are practically nil, unless he is some fortunate individual who inherits a property which has never been shot over and requires organisation from scratch.

The basic rules of partridge driving have been the same from time immemorial, in fact they were practised in the days when coveys were driven into nets by men disguised as horses. I can only suggest that the reader in due time should endeavour to obtain a few of the excellent volumes on partridge driving which have been published periodically from the end of the last century. If he enjoys browsing among secondhand books I recommend that he should procure a few treatises by nimrods such as Stuart-Wortley, Lonsdale, Parker and others, which cover every aspect of shooting on large or modest acreages. Such books nowadays cost only a few pence when discovered on dusty shelves, but those which I have found I treasure more than any other books in my small library.

It is not easy to advise the novice sportsman on how to kill flying birds. Obviously practical experience is far more valuable than verbal generalities.

The partridge is a bird which is quick off the mark and which, unless driven down-wind, will not usually rise to any great height, yet offers a wide variety of shots, particularly as the season wears on. It also presents a small fast-moving target.

Shooting would develop into a poor sport if every shot

was the same, and the copy-book crossing shot with no deviations, to which a few basic rules apply, will seldom be practised when walking up partridges.

The beginner must remember, when lining up on to a flying bird, that he should be looking at his target and not squinting along his barrels as if his shot-gun was a rifle,

and that both eyes, barrel ends and the spot where he intends to place his shot should all be in alignment. Also that the 'swing' on to the bird should automatically begin as he is bringing his gun up to his shoulder and not when it is already there.

Any walked-up partridge has a tendency to fly away from the line, and is likely to be curling and rising to some extent when fired at, even very early in the season. The novice will miss his target below and behind if he does not pay strict attention to impelling a 'lift' to his gun with his left forearm to allow for the extra height and curl which will be gained by the bird between the split second of squeezing the trigger and the pellets reaching it. If his barrel ends do, in fact, cover a rising and curling partridge at the crucial moment of firing he should not miss, and the comparatively simple shot of a partridge going away from him will be mastered, provided always that he does not check his swing as he squeezes the trigger.

It is, of course, of vital importance that the novice should get used to the feel of his gun and ensure that, when it is brought up, the stock becomes part of him and is habitually tucked comfortably against the fleshy pad of his shoulder and not half in his arm-pit for one shot and against his collar-bone—ouch!—for the next. Unless the sportsman's gun feels 'at home' against the shoulder, the alignment will be faulty, and in all probability his shot will be as near the 'middle-stump' as a 'wide' at cricket.

As coveys get wilder and inclined to scatter, there is less time to think and, naturally, the sportsman's brain will not react quickly enough to recall and put into practice what he has read in paragraph umpteen of this or any other book. But the same rules apply to longer shots as those at coveys rising comfortably within range and, unless he is careful, the beginner will very soon develop the undesirable habit of 'poking' his gun. That is, he will get a bit flustered and take snap-shots, fearing that his bird is getting out of range. This will only result in his target and his pellets being just about in the same county and no more!

The novice must, just as with near coveys, swing on to his selected bird, pass over it and follow through according to whether it is rising, curling away or flying low to left or right. He must, though, move and fire faster and, as the range is more extreme, it stands to reason that a longer lead must be given. If he has achieved the correct alignment and is, as he always should be, striving to knock off the partridge's beak his angle and quicker swing on to his target should compensate for the longer range, and not necessitate, as the copy-book sometimes advises, a quick calculation as to how far ahead the shot should be placed!

Certain publications are regularly produced which give a table of lengths of lead required to kill a crossing bird x yards away travelling at y miles an hour. Interesting as such information may be, I would never advise a novice to con it by heart. He has got no time for mental arithmetic when a covey rises forty or forty-five yards away and, even if a lightning mathematician, he would probably check his swing when he reached the estimated distance ahead and miss behind every time! No sportsman has yet been born who can miss a bird in front, so if, instead of filling his head with a lot of science, the novice adopts the golden rules of trying to place his shot in that space just ahead of his target without checking his swing he will have taken his first big stride forward.

There must, as with all sports, be exceptions to the rule, and really fast travellers will sometimes need special treatment. 'The length of a telegraph pole' is often quoted as the lead which should be given to a really screaming covey, which means that the sportsman should be conscious of daylight between his barrel ends and his bird. If that sort of lead has to be given, how much more important it is that the gun should be brought to the shoulder with deadly accuracy.

A partridge offering a crossing or overhead shot to, say, a flank gun is probably travelling at high speed, and may be curling away as well. But the sportsman should grasp the advantage of time. He has seen the covey rise and watched his bird coming towards him. He should avoid the common pitfall of waiting far too long before bringing up his gun, to discover that his bird is upon him by the time he has covered it, leaving him, if he misses, a long difficult second shot which will probably be expensively fruitless.

It is a difficult habit to conquer at first, but the beginner should always endeavour to start his swing when an approaching bird is virtually out of range ahead of him. It will be passing or over him quickly enough, and far better that he should get in a second barrel, if the need arises, when the bird is well within range rather than turn around all anyhow and fling a despairing bunch of pellets at a fast-disappearing speck. I have restricted my remarks to the single bird instead of the covey, because the 'right and left' will be achieved only after experience!

When discussing this book with a friend I suggested that my soundest advice to a beginner when partridge shooting would include aiming in the general direction of a covey, closing both eyes and loosing off both barrels! I was instructed not to be frivolous! The novice sportsman has probably heard of the expression covering such behaviour. It is called 'browning' and is to be discouraged!

THE PHEASANT

Maurice Turner

The Pheasant is a common sight, hanging in poulterers' and butchers' shops throughout the season, and is often a subject for the Christmas card, so I am sure that the reader is familiar with the plumage of the splendid cock bird and his more sombrely dressed lady.

This bird can be traced back in our history for a thousand years. It is not fully known from where it originated, except that it once frequented certain areas of the Black Sea, South-eastern Europe and Asia Minor, where, nowadays, it is probably a fairly rare bird.

The pheasant of today is the result of cross-breeding of the beautiful Old English purple-rumped pheasant and the lighter Chinese ring-necked species, which was brought here at the end of the eighteenth century. Pheasant farms and hatcheries are, nowadays, virtually producing to order such types as have been introduced to these Islands from time to time, and many of the big shoots contain a stock of the 'versicolor', originally a native of Japan. This bird is predominantly a dark glossy green, and is a distinct and somewhat small species which is not to be confused with the very handsome, almost black, melanistic pheasant, which, again, is a feature of some coverts today.

The pheasant mates in the early spring and is polygamous. That is to say the cock is not, as is the partridge, faithful to one wife only. He becomes irritable with his rivals at the beginning of the mating season and quarrels and fights if there are not enough wives to go round, to the detriment of the hen population. For this reason, cocks only are killed and hens spared from about mid-December onwards on properly controlled shoots.

The cock will remain with his harem throughout the breeding season, which begins in April, when the hen lays up to a dozen eggs in a hollow lined with leaves in tall grass or cover usually on dry ground.

The pheasant, essentially a bird of woodland and covert, prefers well-watered areas as its habitat, and is at home even on reedy and marshy land. It ranges afar for its daily ration and, during the day, can be flushed from hedgerows, ditches, bramble patches and fields of stubble, clover, mustard and roots. On a modest acreage with limited woodland the largest proportion of the bag is often obtained from outlying cover rather than from the spinneys and copses themselves.

The pheasant chicks, when they are maturing in the early summer, will learn to seek their own food, which consists of grubs and insects, grain seeds, berries and tender shoots, and will not retain the same family bond of the partridge. A 'nye' of pheasants, like a 'covey' of partridges, is, though, a well-known term denoting a family gathering and, early in the shooting season, a family which has not yet been disturbed may sometimes be flushed with a noisy whirr of wings from the corner of a covert.

In these days more pheasants are bred and shot probably than ever before. The tendency to 'put down' birds has gained in popularity, pheasant rearing has become an industry and farms and hatcheries are now thriving. But putting down pheasants is an expensive luxury which can be practised only by well-subscribed shoots which have keepers, or other such custodians, to tend and watch over their charges. Each bird costs the very minimum of a pound before it is earning its living, so the members of a syndicate must be prepared to dip into their pockets if the natural stock of the shoot is to be increased by such numbers as its size and acreage of woodland can comfortably support.

The beginner, when he has first acquired his few hundred acres, will look forward to his spinneys, copses and hedgerows to provide him with his sport in the autumn and winter. He has seen wild pheasants and hopes that they nest within his boundaries, nevertheless thinks seriously about 'putting down' a few birds. To such a beginner I would advise caution in the hope that he may be saved a few pounds.

Many inexperienced and over-keen sportsmen are under the impression that 'putting down' birds consists of buying pheasant poults, transporting them to the chosen cover, turning them loose, saying 'shoo', then leaving them to fend for themselves until they rise, as magnificent cock pheasants to be downed later in the year. If poults reacted to such treatment and lived to grow strong on the wing more pheasants than ever would be reared! Unfortunately 'putting down' is not as simple as that.

The eggs themselves naturally cost less than the chicks and growing birds, but require old broody hens to take over the business of hatching. But at whatever age the young are procured, coops, kindred equipment and space will have to be obtained and the pheasants fed and nurtured much the same as ordinary barnyard pullets. By mid-summer the poults can be transferred to the chosen covers, but they must be introduced to the wild life by degrees, still fed artificially, enclosed at night and kept safe from marauders. If there is no member of a small shoot who can spare the time to give daily attention to the young birds, then some 'local' will have to be employed and entrusted to do the job conscientiously, which all adds to the cost.

The birds can be left only when they are used to their environment, can forage for themselves and roost in the trees. Even then there is the danger that the novice may have chosen cover which, to all outward appearances, is ideal, but does not 'hold' the birds, which gradually stray away to other woods to somebody else's benefit. He may have selected his area of woodland for his young birds because it is reasonably thickly vegetated and looks attractive. Yet he has not taken into account that it is waterless and isolated, is on top of a hill and open to all the rigours of the British climate and does not produce from its soil nearly enough of the pheasant's natural food.

There is nothing more heart-rending than to wait eagerly for the day when a chosen cover is to be beaten out and, instead of a fine flush of birds as expected, it produces only the odd shot or two from one corner, a lot of blackbirds and an occasional jay or magpie!

I would, then, caution the novice who is a member of, or running, a small rough shoot to beware of the many pitfalls of 'putting down' birds in small spinneys and copses in the hopes that they will stay there to be shot. Unless his cover is ideal holding ground, and the farmer will help by planting out a bit of mustard here and there and grow clover or roots as additional attractions, he is doomed to disappointment.

Shall we suppose, then, that our novice's bit of rough shooting holds a nice little stock of wild birds and that it is now October. He, whose shooting days are limited and precious, will want to pursue the 'long-tail' as soon as legitimately possible. But there are many who contend that the first of October is too early a date for legalised pheasant shooting to start and, indeed, the true sportsman will find little joy in plastering three-quarter-grown

birds which rise flapping a few yards away just because his diary reads on that day, 'Pheasant shooting begins.'

I would recommend that the members of a small syndicate should look to the shorter winter days to provide them with sport, and restrict the first two or three shoots in October and early November to fully fledged cocks only. This may leave only a few weeks during which hens become fair game, but if every pheasant that rises from the first of October onwards is unmercifully fired upon by every gun within range the dwindling strength will become wary, expert runners almost before the leaves are off the trees, and the shooting will have been ruined for the last two months of the season.

Probably the happiest shooting days are those when there is a sprinkling of snow on the ground, a few woodcock are 'in' and an occasional wisp of teal jump out of a wet ditch to give the bag a mixed flavour. Always a fine runner, the wily pheasant will then take some putting up, and will squat tight or double back when hedgerow and ditch and spinney are being proven by our little band of volunteer beaters. A dog is then more of an asset than ever if he is not afraid of thick or prickly undergrowth.

And the pheasant, when he takes to the wing on such cold crisp days, tests the beginner, standing well back from cover, with a variety of shots, whether his target is a steeply climbing curling cock, a hen sneaking low away or, best of all, a bird travelling high and fast overhead with wings outstretched.

Perhaps at this point, I should divert slightly to warn the beginner that the pheasant is full of surprises! Not only does it appear at the most inopportune moments but it seems also to have the uncanny knack of catching the sportsman off his guard! I hate to remember the number of times I have been frustrated with an empty gun either astride a fence or crawling through a wet brambly ditch!

But the pheasant has one saving grace. Unlike the partridge, it advertises its departure from cover with an exciting whirr of pinions and, if a cock, often with a vocal protest as well. The sportsman does, therefore, have some warning of impending action! On the other hand, if being walked-up in root-fields or other such cover it will often sit tight until the sportsman has practically trodden on it. He then gets the fright of his life and, after recovering from near heart failure, probably fires well below a sharply rising, curling target!

We will, however, assume that our beginner is nicely placed for the first time at the end of a spinney, well balanced on level ground with left foot forward and is

awaiting the approach of the beaters. After the little partridge the pheasant, surely, is going to present a larger,
easier, target, and it is with a feeling almost of noncha-
lance that he awaits his quarry. He identifies the sound of
a rising bird, even if a beater did not yell out 'cock
forward', and with gun at the ready, is all prepared—or
so he thinks. There is a 'whoosh' overhead and, quite
unfairly, a cock pheasant has sailed past at some altitude,
to be saluted with one despairing shot which is a mile
wide! After the next warning cry he sees his bird through
the tree-tops ahead and, swiftly recalling the golden rules,
tries to swing on to and past his target. But no—behind
by a yard or two and no time for a second barrel.

By now our sportsman is gaining a healthy respect for
the 'long-tail' and is secretly hoping that a bird or two
may squat in front of him and give him a chance when
the beaters are close. Sure enough, with a lot of fuss, a
hen pheasant rises just ahead, but she is alert and twenty
feet up, curling and gaining momentum, by the time the
beginner's gun is cuddled in to his shoulder. Alas, she
passes over him to fly another day, with shot barely
brushing her tail feathers. A second cartridge is
expended, but the shot is way behind.

I may have over-emphasised the failure of our beginner
to come to terms with his first pheasants, but I have done
my duty if I have convinced him that the size and appar-
ently slower flight of these birds does not make them any
easier to kill than their smaller relations of September
days.

There are, of course, many many exceptions, and the
'flapper' of early October or the bird which rises within
easy range when being walked-up are, to say the least,
targets which should seldom be missed. In fact, many
wretched pheasants are blown to pieces by over-anxious
sportsmen who will not allow them to get more than a
few feet above ground before they are 'plastered'.

It is the pheasant which is on the alert and driven out

of cover which is the hardest to hit, and the higher over-head the bird is, the more satisfactory is the 'thump' when an accurate shot brings it down. But to return to our shoot.

The novice sportsman has, by restraint early in the pheasant season, spared plenty of his birds to fly during those precious winter days which, to the true country-man, have a charm all of their own. He will, also, by then have learnt something about the best way to organise his beats and that a pheasant will squat unseen almost any-where, so that every bit of cover is virtual holding

ground. If his woodland is restricted, then the fields will be worth exploring. Pheasants love kale and roots, although these are often cut or pulled early in the season and, much as the syndicate would wish it, no farmer will give preference to his income from the sale of his shoot-ing rights to delay taking in his crops! But I can well remember the opening day of a modest little syndicate which I had the privilege of joining for under ten pounds. The very first beat through about a quarter of an acre of kale produced six cock pheasants, a hare and a fox!

Pheasants love the sun, and if there are no root crops

left will come out to bask in stubble, clover and grass, so that the odd bird can often be snatched from the most unlikely ground. A good friend and organiser of a rough shoot whom I will call 'Ted' always loosened up his syndicate's leg muscles by starting the day with a broad sweep across plough, grass, stubble, ditches and hedgerow which covered in all about a mile and a half. I christened this manoeuvre 'Ted's fatigue' and, being the shoot's doyen, was invariably the pivot gun! But 'Ted's fatigue' always produced a number of shots, whether they were 'gun-strainers' at partridge, an offering or two at a hare running down the line or, as so often happened, hasty snap-shots loosed off at three or four sun-basking pheasants rising just as the guns had struggled with fire-arms unloaded for safety through a thick hedge! Nevertheless, whatever the weather, 'Ted's fatigue' never lacked surprises from a pheasant or two.

The experience of a big pheasant shoot is something that the beginner will not savour unless he is a fortunate guest gun. The total bag of a big shoot is governed nowadays by the number of pheasants which its acres can maintain and which its keeper can control. The difference between the rough shoot which has so far occupied these pages and the big shoot is as chalk from cheese, and the member of the big syndicate has, virtually, little to do but stand in his allotted place and fire off cartridges. 'Sour grapes,' the reader may say, but one type of shooting occupies the sportsman in the pursuit of a limited amount of wild game, while the other is rather more artificial in that hand-reared birds are shot under strict control and the sportsmen, confronted with driven birds, shoot with the minimum of exercise. 'Nice work if you can get it,' is perhaps the best way of summing up the attractions of expensive syndicate shooting. But the novice sportsman, even though his pocket can stand the strain, is unlikely, unless he is very lucky, to be offered a vacancy in a large established syndicate and have to lay in a stock of No. 6 for his pheasant shooting by the thousand!

I am probably being a hypocrite, as I have had some wonderful days on keepered shoots. Yet, on the whole, my cup has been full on those days towards the end of the season when 'cocks only' is the order of the day and the shoot's extremities are being beaten out and the big coverts left alone.

To write about the killing of the pheasant would be repetitive from other chapters. I might, though, pass on the recommendation of a good and wise man who, after I had been consistently missing tall birds, once told me to say to myself as I brought up my gun: 'Up the smoke trail and shoot his brother in front.' This being translated meant that you followed up imaginary exhaust smoke pouring from a pheasant's tail, swung past the bird and endeavoured to kill an imaginary pheasant flying ahead of the real one. Nine times out of ten I forgot to say this to myself in the excitement of the moment, but, on some occasions when tall pheasants gave me time to put this maxim into practice, I found that my percentage of 'head-and-neck' hits began to increase. It is, as has already been written in this book, a virtual impossibility to miss in front, even though every sportsman strives to place his shot in that open space just in front of the bird's beak. So if, when confronted with overhead or crossing birds, the beginner can adopt the practice of trying to 'shoot his brother in front' he may find that he is squeezing his trigger when his barrel ends are just that fraction farther forward and thus improve his aim.

I must stop lest I confuse the novice with too much science and reluctantly close this chapter on that most wonderful of birds, Phasianus Colchicus.

DEER

Maurice Turner

To the beginner the mention of deer will probably conjure up visions of Euston Station and the Scottish Highlands. Perhaps the sportsman's greatest achievement in the British Isles is the stalking and killing in Scotland of the 'Royal', the Red Stag carrying antlers with twelve points. I have spoken with several nimrods who have stalked deer in Scotland, and asked them for the best advice I could offer to a beginner. The reply has always been the same: 'Tell him never to attempt to stalk his first few deer alone.'

But shall we forget the Scottish deer forests for the moment and consider these animals in a general way. There are four main wild species with which the novice sportsman will become familiar if he makes a study of deer. These are the Red, Sika, Fallow and Roe. There are one or two other feral species which have wandered outside parks, but with these we need not be concerned, as they are rarities. The beginner, nowadays, need never look far to find deer, as they colonise most big estates and are on the increase in very many forests, so much so that the Forestry Commission has had to appoint keepers or, for want of a better name, stalkers in many parts of the country to keep the deer population under control.

Deer are not 'choosey' eaters, and will have a go at most succulent new growths, even raiding flower gardens at night and wrecking shrubs. Many, because of this habit, get fired upon indiscriminately and out of season, regardless of sex, and suffer severe or light wounds according to the fire-arm employed. Also, a lot of damage is attributed to deer when the miscreants are, in fact, other animals, and they sometimes get unnecessarily persecuted accordingly.

The Red Deer are easily distinguished by their height and length—a stag stands nearly four feet at the shoulder—and by their antlers, which often carry more than twelve points in parkland herds. The beginner could, possibly, confuse the Red and Sika deer, except that the

latter are smaller, darker coated and spotted, and it is
rare for their antlers to carry more than eight points.

The Fallow are noted for their heavily white-spotted
coats, and the bucks have palmated antlers. They are
very common in parks. They are smaller than the Red
Deer, and a buck's shoulder height is about three feet.

The Roe, the smallest of our deer, is a shy and retiring
little fellow, not so often seen in semi-captivity. It stands
about two feet high and appears to be tail-less. The
buck's antlers are limited to six points, and the bases are
rough. This is called 'pearling'.

It may interest the reader to learn that the male and
female of the Red and Sika deer are known as 'stags' and
'hinds' respectively, while those of the Fallow and Roe
are called 'bucks' and 'does'. Also horns which are shed
should be referred to as 'antlers', horns being permanent
growths such as on cattle and goats!

Our deer all shed old and grow new antlers from
spring until late summer except for the Roe, which casts
his in late autumn. This last is an odd habit, because a
good growth of antler depends largely on plentiful food,
and the Roe buck grows his pair during the rigours of
winter.

The novice sportsman, wishing to shoot an English
deer, will probably be able to obtain permission, if he
applies very diplomatically, from the owner of a deer-
infested forest. The Forestry Commission employ their
own staff, and will not grant licences to shoot deer on any
of their land for which shooting rights have not been
granted.

The forest-owner will give his blessing only if the
novice sportsman is abiding by the Deer Act of 1963 and
can convince him that he has practised enough with
his weapon to kill outright, and not just wound his
deer.

The Deer Act of 1963 decrees, among other things,
that:

(a) No smooth-bore gun smaller than a 12 bore shall be used.

(b) No cartridge loaded with shot smaller than S.S.G. (not less than diameter 0.269 in.) shall be used.

(c) No rifle having a calibre of less than 0.240 in. or a muzzle energy of less than 1,700 foot pounds shall be used.

(d) Only a soft-nosed or hollow-nosed bullet shall be used.

(e) Deer shall not be killed between the expiration of the first hour after sunset and the commencement of the last hour before sunrise.

Close seasons do, of course, have to be observed, which are:

(a) From 1st May to 31st July for stags and bucks (except roe deer).

(b) From 1st March to 31st October for all hinds and does.

Scotland has different close seasons, which are 21st October to 30th June for stags, and 16th February to 20th October for hinds.

It is possible that the novice's host is proud of his deer population, and will only allow the shooting of beasts which are going back (nine to twelve years old or more according to breed and locality) or do not carry prime heads. In this case the novice would almost certainly be superintended. But we will assume that our beginner is turned loose on his own and is all keyed up and ready to shoot a fine stag. First, he must realise that deer which have become completely naturalised are the most timid animals in the forest. The novice may think that he is progressing with impeccable stealth, but is quite oblivious to the noises being created by pheasants, jays, magpies, black-birds, grey squirrels and other forest denizens, all of whom are conspiring to advertise his approach.

Equally, he may be creeping about without first ascertaining that he is in a part of the forest where deer abound. They, like any other animals, leave signs of their presence, and before he so much as thinks of a shot, the novice should look for droppings, imprints, cropped grass and foliage, trodden deer paths and so on. He should also listen for deer noises, unmistakable grunts and bellows or, what in some localities is known as 'groaning'. Then having satisfied himself that there are at least some deer

about, he should decide whether to locate his quarry and endeavour to stalk it (much the most commendable method) or indulge in what the Americans call 'still' hunting, which is to wait for the quarry to come to him.

This may need a little preparation, as it is preferable to sit twelve or fifteen feet above ground and, because quiet and the stillness of death is essential, an improvised seat of, say, a piece of plank is desirable. Even when satisfactorily settled down, the novice sportsman must still remember that there are birds and beasts which can give his position away and that, however persistent are the gnats, he must not move a muscle! Hinds will often precede the much coveted stag, and an ill-timed movement, just when deer are coming into view, may send them all scurrying away before a shot can be fired.

Before we go to Scotland perhaps we should consider the selection of our weapon and some essential equipment. I would strongly advise the beginner to forget his shot-gun, unless he is invited to take part in a drive organised for the reduction of the general deer population in a specified forest or of hinds in particular. The range of a shot-gun is extremely limited, it is virtually useless for stalking and the novice sportsman could easily be tempted into taking long shots which only wound and do not kill outright.

The choice of a rifle must obviously depend on the pocket of the individual, and the chances of deer stalking or hunting which are likely to come his way. The price range can vary from as little as fifteen pounds for a converted army-type weapon to as much as two hundred and fifty pounds for a hand-made de luxe rifle. Cogswell & Harrison, for instance, produce a quite serviceable ·303 for about fifteen pounds and other weapons of various bores from ·243 to ·308, ranging in price from about thirty pounds to a hundred pounds.

Personal preference, weight and bank balance all play their part, and whatever his price limitation, the beginner should take time over his purchase, try out one or two weapons and, in consultation with his gunsmith, finally make his choice.

He should, though, not be deluded into thinking that he is to be more admired if he pursues deer with a light-calibre rifle. We cannot all be 'dead-eye Dicks', and the beginner who is only an average shot because he gets only limited practice will stop a beast with a heavy-bore rifle if the shot is somewhat inaccurate, whereas a light bore might inflict only a wound. It does not matter in the least if a heavy-velocity soft-nosed bullet makes a bit of a mess of a pound or two of venison. Far better that than a wretched beast should perish miserably, possibly of thirst.

Though not an essential piece of equipment, a telescopic sight can be a good investment, provided always that it is treated with respect, does not encourage the beginner to take shots at much over a hundred yards and is fitted with precision. It has its limitations, though, as it mists over in the variable weather frequently encountered in the mountains, when the sportsman has to rely on open sights. Foreign makes are now on the British market and, depending on its origin, a serviceable telescopic sight will cost from twenty pounds.

The beginner has the choice of a telescope or a pair of binoculars. One or other is essential when stalking not only to spot deer but also to select a shootable stag when a herd is sighted.

I would advise binoculars, because, although less powerful than a telescope, they are far more manageable and do not have to be rested when in use. If the sportsman is stalking on bare hillsides in Scotland, then it is almost certain that his accompanying ghillie or stalker will have his own cherished instrument, but this must not discourage the beginner from finding deer for himself. A good pair of binoculars, again depending on origin, will cost from twenty pounds.

Perhaps ten or fifteen pounds should be set aside for etceteras such as knife, ammunition, rifle cover, sling and so on.

The novice deer-stalker should not fit himself out with brand-new clothes for his first appearance in Scotland! On his first day out he is quite likely to get wet, and dry off a dozen times, so an old but serviceable suit of plus fours is to be recommended. Brown is the best colour, as this will blend with most types of scenery, but any tweed that is not too startling to behold will probably suffice. Boots rather than shoes are preferable as providing ankle support on uneven ground.

Knee-breeches should be avoided, as they remain clammy and cloying. A waterproof becomes a nuisance in a wind, and can subscribe to noise during a tricky stalk. There is nothing wrong, though, with a waterproof jacket instead of a coat, except that if the sportsman works up a 'rare muck sweat' he is apt to remain uncomfortably sticky within his jacket.

And now for the all-important problem of, as Mrs. Beeton might put it, 'catching your deer'. The vast majority of those who would stalk the Scottish Red deer will be in the same position as those who would shoot the grouse, and look upon such sport as an annual holiday event.

'The old order changeth', and many 'lairds' in the past few years have been forced to let their forests after, in a number of cases, dividing them into smaller shooting areas. Hotels have taken over tenancies for their guests, which has put deer-stalking within the scope of many more sportsman than in years gone by. But it is still an expensive sport, as apart from the initial outlay for arms and equipment, there are costly journeys involved, board and lodging to be paid and the not inconsiderable cost of a day's or week's stalking.

The newcomer to a deer forest in Scotland will know nothing of the lay of the land and the tricks of the wind, and so will be dependent on an accompanying stalker or ghillie or both. He will need a pony and a man to tend it, for the transport of any dead beasts, so there are wages to be paid before he has even set foot on the hill.

It is possible to rent certain grazing land which holds deer for, possibly, thirty pounds a week, but this would not include stalkers, ghillies, ponies or bed and board, the arrangement for which would be somewhat chancy and irksome at long range. If lucky, the beginner might be put in touch with somebody who would lay on all arrangements for him, in which case he might get a fair return for his money by killing half a dozen beasts.

For everything 'laid on', the weekly charge including lodging would work out at a hundred pounds or more for a deer forest, but landlords infinitely prefer a season's tenancy. There is, nevertheless, always the chance that the lessee for a season would be prepared to sub-let for a limited period. This, though, might be only a last-minute arrangement.

As a hotel guest, the beginner is far less dependent on his own organisation, and he has the advantage of a hot bath, comfort and service to which to return after a hard day. The total outlay for hotel shooting may be more, as, apart from board and lodging and tips, not only to hotel staff but to shooting staff also, the daily charge for stalking might well be ten pounds, with the hotel keeping the venison. But this charge will include personnel and pony and, with a reputation to maintain, the hotel manager will probably employ good stalkers or ghillies.

If the sportsman meets with success and returns to the same forest year after year there may come a time when he wishes to stalk alone. This I consider to be inadvisable, and a deer-stalker should never go out unaccompanied. Accidents are frequent in the hills, and if a sportsman falls and injures himself his calls for help may fall on deaf ears, and when found he may be beyond human aid. If he must stalk alone then, at the very least, he should tell some responsible person exactly where he proposes to go.

In any event, if he kills a stag all by himself it has got to be brought down to base, which may cause a number of people a lot of unnecessary inconvenience late in the day. So if he sets out with the intention of killing a stag the deer-stalker might just as well take with him whatever help may ultimately be needed, however experienced he has become.

The beginner, then, if looking forward to stalking his 'Royal', must be prepared to meet such expenses as his trophy will incur, as well as the cost of mounting the head! I can in a short space give only a rough idea of outlay, and the newcomer to stalking is the only one who can ultimately make the important decision on how much to invest. And there I must leave him, except to say that advertisements in sporting papers should be studied, the editors of which are usually most helpful with advice on when and where to go.

And please, when you have acquired your rifle, read, remember and practise the safety rules, even when you may seem to have the world to yourself. A rifle bullet can be lethal at very long range, and there are shepherds and crofters on hills and foresters in woodland who are no better off for lumps of lead in vital places!

INDEX